FRANK BURTON MILLER

SOLDIERS AND SAILORS

OF THE

PLANTATION OF LOWER ST. GEORGES
MAINE

Who Served In The War For American Independence

BY FRANK BURTON MILLER

Member of the Maine Historical Society

CLEARFIELD

Originally published
Rockland, Maine, 1931

Reprinted for
Clearfield Company, Inc. by
Genealogical Publishing Co., Inc.
Baltimore, Maryland
1999

International Standard Book Number: 0-8063-4924-7

Made in the United States of America

FOREWORD

As is locally known, I have been engaged for several years in collecting material for a history of the Plantation of Lower St. Georges, in the Province of Maine, now known as the towns of Cushing and St. George. Having acquired considerable information regarding the genealogical history of the early settlers in this region, and the part they played in civil and military affairs, I am, of late, receiving many inquiries from the descendants of these families, whether or not they are eligible to membership in the "Societies of the Sons or the Daughters of the American Revolution." To save time and labor in answering each individual inquiry, I have prepared a record of the naval and military service of those men, numbering about one hundred, who contributed their part, humble as it may have been, to make the thirteen Colonies free and independent States, and to the severance of all political allegiance to Great Britain. Whenever possible I have expanded these sketches, as here appears, by adding material of a public, private and family nature. By so doing, many of the subjects of these sketches can be more easily identified. As to those whom I am endeavoring to rescue from the realms of oblivion, they having lived in the dim and misty past, errors are bound to creep in. If such errors are detected, either by the casual reader, or the descendants of these men of courage and action, it will be appreciated by the writer to be so informed for correction in future editions of this record.

THE ST. GEORGES RIVER

St. Georges river which bisected the plantation of Lower St. Georges and is referred to many times in the foregoing sketches of Revolutionary Soldiers and Sailors, is becoming better known and more appreciated as the years go by. It possesses history worthy of continued study and patient investigation. Since its discovery by Waymouth, three hundred and twenty-five years ago, many events of interest and importance have been its heritage. On its shores was erected the first cross of British occupation

FOREWORD

in this region, and close to that historic spot Major Gen. Henry Knox, the friend and counsellor of Washington, came to spend his remaining days "far from the madding crowd's ignoble strife." Along its wooded slopes and by its quiet waters, British stubborness gave way to American valor in the Revolutionary struggle. From its hillsides, fort and garrison house dealt out leaden rain and iron hail. Along its banks Wawenock and Tarrantine struggled for mastery and occupation. On its eastern side the lilies of France contended for a season, but in vain, with the cross of St. George, for dominion and power in this region. Contending forces have disturbed its quietness and serenity. Across its waters War has sounded his tocsin, and Peace has chanted her victories. Such are the fragments to be gathered up, and cast into the urn of history.

> "Smile on, fair river, flowing to the sea,
>   And chant, O sea, your anthem evermore;
> Seasons shall roll, and human life shall be
>   Golden with hope as life hath been before;
> The sacred records of the dead remain,
>   And faithful history calls them from the past;
> Their feet shall tread with ours the distant plain,
>   Whose shining space outspreads sublime and vast."

FRANK B. MILLER

FRANK B. MILLER, Judge of the Rockland Municipal Court, died November 28, 1930, in his sixty-ninth year, and while these sketches were being brought out in their present form.

MAINE SOLDIERS AND SAILORS

··o◆o··

ADAMS, RICHARD. He was commissioned captain July 2, 1778, of the 9th company of Colonel Wheaton's 4th Lincoln county regiment, his name being listed among the officers of the Massachusetts militia.

Richard Adams was born at Plymouth, Mass., June 14, 1719, and died in Cushing, August, 1795. His wife, Mary Carver, was born in Plymouth, September 14, 1721, died in Cushing in 1796. Both are buried on Garrison island, Friendship. He was a blacksmith by trade and lived in Kingston, Mass., until about the year 1752. From the records of that town it appears he subsequently became a resident of Wareham. He removed to Newport, Rhode Island, where he remained about two years and thence removed to Maine with his friends the Bradfords and Robinsons, during the mania which prevailed at the time for adventure in this region.

He located in the plantation of Meduncook, now the town of Friendship, but the exact year of his coming to Meduncook cannot now be stated. From the early records of the plantation, it appears that Captain Adams was elected an assessor in 1769, and reelected in 1770, 1771, 1772, 1774, 1782, 1783, 1786, 1787 and 1788. He was chosen collector of taxes in 1784, and a member of the Committee of Safety in 1776. He was elected captain of the local militia in 1775. On October 30, 1771, Isaac Winslow, Thomas Fluker and Francis Waldo, administrators of the estate of Samuel Waldo, conveyed to Richard Adams the premises on which he lived in Friendship, until his removal to Cushing about 1789. Mr. Adams' name appears as a resident of Cushing in the census of 1790.

At the annual plantation meeting held March 18, 1771, it was voted that Richard Adams and others "with submission to Providence, will appear on the sixteenth of April next, at the ministerial lot, in order to fence the marsh, at nine o'clock in the morning, if the weather be good, otherwise the first day ensuing." On the day appointed Mr. Adams, with seventeen others, met at the ministerial lot and searched out the line between it and the lot adjoining on the northeast side of it, fenced the salt marsh, and let it for the year's crop to Joshua Collamore, Ebenezer Morton, Joshua Morton and Micajah Drinkwater for two pounds and fourteen pence. On December 17, 1771, Mr. Adams in the presence of John Demorse and Micajah Drinkwater, warned Richard Starling "to depart the house and relinquish possession of the ministerial lot according to the tenor of the lease by which he went on the lot and into the house June 28, 1770." The committee reported, "that said Starling met them, at the same time abusing them with scurrilous language and unusual behavior, shutting them out of doors and ringing a cow bell."

The will of Mr. Adams, dated August 27, 1792, was probated September 19, 1797, and was witnessed by Thurston Whiting, Jacob Graffam and John Short. He appointed his sons Richard, Thomas and George as executors. Thomas Adams having deceased, letters testamentary were issued to Richard and George Adams, mariners, both of Cushing, September 19, 1797. Moses Copeland and Joseph Copeland, both of Cushing, qualified as sureties on their official bond. Mr. Adams bequeathed to his wife Mary during her natural life, the south-east front room in his dwelling house together with the kitchen, oven and well; his best feather bed with all necessary appurtenances to the same; all necessary furniture for one room; necessary kitchen utensils; one good cow to be kept both summer and winter; fire wood brought to her door and cut for the chimney during her life; fifteen bushels bread corn of different kinds; flax and wool annually sufficient to keep her bedding and clothing in repair; a sufficient annual supply of potatoes and vegetables, tea, coffee and sweetening and other necessaries. To his daughters Sela Baker, Margaret Gray and Hope Davis he gave one cow each; to his daughters Hope Davis and Lucy Graham six shillings each, and his household furniture to be equally divided among them; to his granddaughters Polly Baker, Polly Bradford and Polly Adams, daughters of his son Richard, one tablespoon apiece; to his son Richard all his wearing apparel; to his grandson Richard his large pair of gold sleeve buttons; to his grandson Robert Davis, son of his daughter Hope, his small pair of gold sleeve buttons; to his sons Richard, Thomas and George his homestead premises, stock, farming tools and implements, Crotch Island, situated near his farm on Meduncook river, and the remainder of his estate to be equally divided among them.

On November 21, 1775, the local Committee of Correspondence petitioned the General Court of the Province of Massachusetts for assistance to protect the citizens and to defend the plantation of Meduncook from British assaults. The petitioners set forth "that whereas we are in danger of enemies as much as other places, although the good Providence of God had hitherto protected us, blessed be His name, yet we count it our duty to use the best means we can for our safety and defense, and in order thereunto we think it necessary to have Military Officers among us, to which we did expect some help from Col. Cargill, but have not so yet received it, and so are destitute of Commanders.

"Whereupon a very considerable part of our people have made choice of Mr. Richard Adams for the Captain, and Mr. Jonah Gay for their Lieutenant, and Mr. Jesse Thomas for their Ensign, and we, the Committee, do approve of their choice and do judge the aforesaid gentlemen fit and proper for said places, and we in behalf of the aforesaid people and ourselves, do humbly pray this Honorable Court to send commissions to the aforesaid Gentlemen, accordingly that we may not be as sheep without a shepherd, and your petitioners as in duty bound will ever pray."

It is difficult at this late day to collect many facts concerning the personal appearance and mental endowments of Captain Adams. His great grandson, the late Raymond C. Davis, has paid him this tribute:

"Richard Adams was a stout, fleshy man, kind and social. His voice was strong and cheerful, so say the old people. By conversing with the aged of the days when they were young, my mind has been led to dwell intensely on the times and associates of old Richard. I have stood on the turf that covers his grave, and in imagination have conjured him up from the grave, and his life from the past. Ah! he and those of his generation were *manly* men—they were brave men, for they gave life and blood for a free land—they were wise men, for they bequeathed liberty and its blessings to their children—they were good men, for their prayers secured a blessing from God."

James Adams of Washington, D. C., his grandson, wrote of him as follows:

[7]

"I have heard him spoken of as a man of intelligence, of enterprise and means and of some note among his contemporaries. I recollect once making the casual inquiry of a person who knew my grandfather, as to what sort of a man he was, and his quaint reply was this: 'He was the *knowinest* man about these part.' "

It is quite evident that he was a worthy man, and held in high esteem by his acquaintances and townsmen.

ADAMS, THOMAS. He enlisted in Capt. Philip M. Ulmer's company, Col. McCobb's regiment, on an expedition to the Penobscot, July 8, 1779, and was discharged September 24, 1779.

Mr. Adams was one of the three sons of Capt. Richard Adams, but did not survive his father, dying between the years 1792 and 1797. Mr. Adams' son Thomas was a resident of Newburyport, Massachusetts, at the time of his death. By the terms of his will probated in Suffolk county Probate Court on the first Tuesday of July, 1849, Mr. Adams ordered his property to be divided into ten parts, two of which were to be expended under the direction of the "American Board of Commissioners for Foreign Missions for Christianizing the Jews, the descendants of Abraham."

ALLEN, JOHN. He served as a private in Capt. Archibald McAllister's company, Col. Samuel McCobb's regiment, on the expedition against Majorbagaduce from July 11, 1779, to Sept. 24, 1799, when he was discharged.

Mr. Allen resided on St. Georges island, now known as Allen island, and dying intestate his widow Keturah was appointed administratrix September 8, 1790. His estate was inventoried at 39 pounds, 14 shillings and 4 pence on Oct. 17, 1789, by Dunbar Henderson, Eleazer Gay and John Barter, the appraisers. Eleazer Gay and Dunbar Henderson were appointed commissioners to examine claims against the estate, and filed their account in Lincoln county Probate Court, Sept. 18, 1792.

ANNIS, JOHN. He was born July 20, 1732; married Mary Maloney of Cushing, a daughter of Walter Maloney. He came from Boston to Broad cove, prior to 1760, and bought the farm numbered 39, now owned and occupied by the heirs of the late Charles H. Freeman. He remained in possession until April 17, 1779, when he sold his interest in the same to Abijah Waterman of Waldoboro, and removed to Warren.

Shortly after his removal to Warren, he was shot while engaged in privateering. Besides the regular garrison at St. Georges fort, the stone garrison in Cushing, and the block house at Pleasant Point, a company of rangers, of which Capt. Annis was a member, scouting to the eastward, was on pay from June 19, to Nov. 30, 1755. His wife was born June 7, 1736. She married a Blaisdell for her second husband and resided many years on Blaisdell's island, but died in Camden. Their children:

1. Amy, born July 19, 1754. In early womanhood she removed to Boston but for some unexplained reason she held no communication with her relatives. She never married.

2. Susannah, born Sept. 28, 1756, married Samuel Boggs, 3d; resided in Warren and died Nov. 15, 1838. He was born in 1759 in the old fort at Pemaquid; resided at the old homestead, Warren; and died October 1, 1834.

3. Mary, born Oct. 11, 1759; married Alexander Bird of Cushing.

4. John, 2d, born November 8, 1761; married a Cleverly, or Caverly, and removed to Boston.

5. Hannah, born June 1, 1764; died Sept. 15, 1840.

6. Thomas, born October 5, 1766.

7. Samuel, born March 4, 1769; married Sarah Thorndike, and removed to Camden, according to Eaton. Records of Cushing show his intentions of marriage to Joanna Gerrish of Cushing were filed June 12, 1790.

8. Martha, born January 24, 1772; removed to and died in Boston.

9. Sarah, born Jan. 4, 1774; married John Thorndike; resided in Camden and died Dec. 12, 1867, being burned to death in her bed.

10. James Caldor, born Nov. 16, 1776. He was lost at sea.

BARTER, JOHN. He served as a private in Capt. Archibald McAllister's company, attached to Col. Samuel McCobb's regiment, in the expedition against Majorbagaduce, now Castine, serving from July 11, 1777, to Sept. 24, 1777.

In Greene's History of Boothbay, Mr. Barter is listed as a soldier from that town. According to the census of 1790, he resided on the east side of St. Georges river, his family consisting of nine members.

BRAZIER, JOHN. He enlisted as a private in Capt. Ludwig's company at Waldoboro, October 7, 1777, and was discharged December 22, 1777. The company was raised for the defense of Machias.

Although Mr. Brazier was a resident of Cushing in 1790 it is probable that he was living in Meduncook plantation at the time of his enlistment, as he joined with several of its inhabitants in a petition to Thomas Hutchinson—"Captain General and Governor-in-Chief in and over His Majesty's Province of Massachusetts Bay, in New England, and His Majesty's Council and the House of Representatives,"—protesting against the proposal of the inhabitants of the lower part of St. Georges river to be incorporated in a township with them. The petitioners objected to the proposed union. . . "for besides divers reasons that may be given, we are also discommodiously situated in respect of them that we can never be accommodated with one meeting house, so as women and children can go to meeting at all, and men but seldom." On the same day Mr. Brazier signed a similar petition addressed to Thomas Flucker, royal secretary of Colonial Massachusetts.

Mr. Brazier was chosen one of the hog reeves of Cushing in 1793 and 1794. The position requires a trained hand to catch and hold the elusive pig.

On March 21, 1768, Mr. Brazier caused to be recorded, in the office of the plantation clerk, the names and date of birth of his children, as follows: William, born March 20, 1761; Bathsheba, born January 9, 1763; Nathan, born October 17, 1765; Ruth, junior, born November 5, 1767; John, junior, born June 12, 1769. On May 24, 1773, the boy Nathan became lost in the woods and was never found.

BRISON, JOHN. He enlisted as a private in Capt. Philip M. Ulmer's company, Col. McCobb's regiment, serving from July 8, 1779, to September 24, 1779, as a member of the Penobscot expedition.

Mr. Brison conveyed his farm, numbered 24 in the allotment of lands made by Gen. Waldo to the early settlers, to Daniel Collins, Oct. 10, 1792, for 100 pounds. The farm contained 100 acres, and is situated on the west side of St. Georges river. It was bounded on the north by lot No. 23, belonging to the heirs of Thomas Saunders, and on the south by the Meeting House lot. The Collins farm is now owned by Dr. Oram R. Lawry of Rockland and occupied by him as a summer residence. During the war of 1812-1814 a British vessel sailed up St. Georges river and proceeded to seize and destroy considerable shipping on both sides of the river. One of the vessels, called the Fair Trader, belonging to Capt. Andrew Robinson, anchored in Collins cove, was set on fire and destroyed.

BRISON, WILLIAM. He enlisted as a private in Capt. Samuel Gregg's company, Col. James Cargill's regiment, August 25, 1775, and was discharged December 31, 1775. The company was stationed at St. Georges, Waldoboro and Camden for the defense of the sea coast.

BROWN, JOHN. He enlisted as a private in Capt. Benjamin Lemont's company, Major Lithgow's detachment of militia, Sept. 15, 1779. He was a member of the Penobscot expeditionary forces until Nov. 1, 1779, when he was discharged.

Mr. Brown was a resident of Cushing prior to 1760, and either owned or occupied lot No. 40, situated on the western side of St. Georges river, now owned by the present writer.

He was probably a descendant of the John Brown mentioned by Eaton in his Annals of Warren. There were about this time (1635), or a little later, says Eaton, 84 families, besides fishermen, residing between the Kennebec and St. Georges, namely: 20 near Sagadahoc, 31 east of that river to Merry-meeting bay, 6 from Cape Newagen to Pemaquid, 10 at New Harbor, and 2 at St. Georges, besides those farther "within land," at Sheepscot and Damariscotta. The two at St. Georges, denominated "farmers," were said to be Mr. Foxwell, on the west side, at Saquid Point, and Philip Swaden, or Snowden, on the east side of Quisquamego. John Brown, also, of New Harbor, not long after this period, claimed land at the mouth of St. Georges river, at a place called Sawkhead. To what places these names refer cannot now, perhaps, be ascertained. Possibly Quisquamego may have been the high ridge between the bay at Thomaston and the Westkeag river, called by the present Penobscots, "Quesquitcumegek," or "high carrying-place." Saquid, pronounced with the a broad as in Saco, was probably the same as Sawkhead; and both appear to have been the ancient name of Pleasant Point in Cushing, still called, we believe, by the Penobscot Indians, "Sunkheath." This point, situated at the mouth of the river, answers to Brown's description of Sawkhead, and is probably the oldest farm in this region, having been cultivated for nearly 300 years.

BURTON, BENJAMIN. In the list of officers of the Massachusetts militia dated at St. Georges, June 3, 1776, appears the name of Benjamin Burton as 1st lieutenant of Capt. George Young's 5th company, Col. Mason Wheaton's 4th Lincoln county regiment. His commission is dated July 3, 1776. He was also 2d lieutenant in Capt. Samuel King's company, Col. Thomas Marshall's regiment. Rations were allowed from date of service, December 3, 1776, to Feb. 21, 1777, was credited with eighty days allowance and for eleven days travel on march from Boston to Bennington. Mr. Burton was captain in Col. Henry Sherburn's regiment and as such paid accounts for service from January 1, 1777, to June 3, 1779. He resigned June 3, 1779, having enlisted for three years. The army reports show that he served three months and ten days as lieutenant in Col. Marshall's regiment, and twenty-five months and twenty-three days as captain in Col. Sherburn's regiment. He later served under Brig. Gen. Wadsworth. His final military service covered the period from April 20, 1781, to Nov. 20, 1781.

On June 4, 1930, Hattie C. Burton conveyed to the Mackay Radio and Telegraph Co., Inc., the Col. Burton homestead premises, containing 117 acres, situated on the western side of St. Georges river, in the town of Cushing. The sale of a Maine farm seldom excites more than ordinary local interest, and many times hardly that. The Burton family having played an important part in civil and military activities in the Colonial history of the District of Maine, gives this farm an outstanding position when compared with other Maine homesteads. The material which comprises the following sketch of Col. Burton has been gathered from various sources—family records and traditions, writings of local historians, and an extended contribution by Joseph Williamson to the Maine Historical Society.

Benjamin Burton was born in the old block-house in Thomaston, Maine, on the ninth of December, 1749. He resided the greater part of his life four miles below that place, in the town of Cushing, and died at Warren, May 23, 1835, aged eighty-five years. His grandfather, of the same name, was native of Wales, and was in Cromwell's army when he reduced the Irish to obedience under the Commonwealth. His son Benjamin, at the age of twenty-one years, was induced to emigrate to the Province of Maine, by General Waldo's Proclamation, which young Burton had seen, and which offered lands in the Waldo Patent, without price, to actual settlers. He embarked with his father and many others, and landed at St. Georges river, in 1736. His father died during the passage. In the celebrated expedition against Louisburg, in 1745, the son was a lieutenant, and as such acquired considerable credit. On his return, the command of the block-house at St. Georges, now Thomaston, was assigned him, Jabez Bradbury being at the same time captain of the fort, and prior to hostilities, which in August of that year were declared against all the tribes, being also truck-master.

In the following month a large body of the Tarratine Indians, who were probably not aware of the declaration, encamped in the vicinity of the fort, to which they sent four principal chiefs or sagamores, who had assumed English military titles, to procure ammunition. Struck with the perilous condition of these visitants, who were until then apparently ignorant of their danger, Bradbury ordered them to return directly to their companions, or they were dead men. But either through fatigue, or more probably an intemperate use of strong drink, they encamped on the margin of Mill river for the night. Learning their position, Captain Burton and Lieutenant Proctor of the militia, with a band of men, pursued and found them in their camp. One, whose name has not been preserved, having stepped down to the river for water, escaped. Burton, with a single blow of his sword, cut off the head of Captain Morris, one of the chiefs. Captain Sam, another one, was dispatched by Proctor, or some of the party. Colonel Job was taken prisoner and carried to Boston, where he died in confinement. Some regretted the event so early in the war, and so exasperating to the Tarratines. Others rejoiced, especially at the death of Morris, for "he had been a great terror" to the settlers. The son of Morris, in revenge for his father's death, frequently threatened to kill Burton, but never found an opportunity to execute his purpose.

After the treaty of Aix-la-Chapelle, in 1749, it was supposed that the war had terminated, and that the settlement at Broadbay, Waldoboro, would be revived. The next spring, therefore, one Smith, a German, against the remonstrances of Burton and other friends, returned with his wife and her son to their old habitation in that place. His removal being known, he was followed by Indians, who soon attacked his cabin, and by hurling torches against the roof, which was covered with spruce bark, endeavored to set it on fire. All such as took effect, Smith was able from the inside to thrust off, and thus avert the intended mischief. Unable to succeed in this manner, the savage assailants resorted to stratagem, by cowering down in silence and entirely out of sight. Smith, finding the attack had ceased, raised his head through the roof, when he received a ball in his neck. The Indians then rushed into the hut, dispatched his wife and himself, and scalped them. Her son, Peter Canagh, who was lame, having been hidden in the cellar, was not injured, and afterwards returned safely to the fort.

When the war had fully closed, about the year 1750-1, Burton settled in the present town of Cushing. Being a man of prudence, and fearing that peace would not continue, he judiciously and strongly fortified his habitation, whereby it acquired the name of "Burton's fort." Although always watchful of danger, he made a comfortable living for his family by cultivating potatoes, which with fish and clams constituted their chief means of support. In the French and sixth Indian war, which commenced in 1754, an expedient, adopted during the preceding one, and which proved effective, was now pursued to great advantage and extent. When any of the men went from the fort, they were flanked by some half dozen Newfoundland dogs, which were trained to keep at the distance of a gun-shot from the party, in order to surprise any Indian lurking about or in the ambush. Through fear of detection, the dogs would rarely be fired upon, while they always gave the men timely warning to defend themselves against any Indians whom they might scent. At one time when an alarm was given, Captain Burton and his wife, with four children, were at some distance from the fort. Taking one child on his back, and one under each arm, his wife carrying a fourth, they all reached their home in safety. This worthy man was frozen to death, March 21, 1762, by being caught in the ice in the St. Georges river, while in a boat. The snow was at that time four feet deep on the ground and covered with a crust sufficiently solid to bear teams.

Such was the father of Benjamin Burton, the third of that name, who is the principal subject of this note and intended biographical sketch. He was left an orphan at the early age of thirteen. On the memorable sixteenth of December, 1773, happening to be in Boston on a visit, he went in the crowd to the Old South Meeting-house. As soon as the patriot orator had closed his animated address, Burton heard the cry of "Tea party, tea party!" Touched with the spirit of the times, he joined in the enterprise, went on board one of the ships, and labored with his might between two and three hours in assisting to throw three cargoes of the detested tea into the water. The whole number of chests broken open and emptied was 342. It being about low water, the tea rested on the bottom, and when the tide rose, it floated and was lodged by the surf along the shores.

In September, 1776, Mr. Burton was commissioned a lieutenant in the Continental army, and the following spring he received the appointment of captain in Colonel Thurburn's regiment in Rhode Island. Withdrawing from the service, July 14, 1779, he returned to his home in Cushing. From April, 1780, he served as major about nine months in Maine, under General Peleg Wadsworth, grandfather of Henry Wadsworth Longfellow, Maine's famous poet, and was discharged only a few days before that intrepid officer was taken prisoner and carried to Bagaduce (now Castine), on the 18th of February, 1781. By order of the British commander at that post, a flag of truce was sent to Camden, at Wadsworth's request, carrying letters from him to his wife and to Governor Hancock, which were forwarded by Major Burton, then at Camden.

After Burton's return home, and after he had conducted the General's wife and her friend, Miss Fenno, under a passport, to visit him in his confinement, the vessel of Burton was captured by the enemy near Monhegan. He was immediately conveyed to Bagaduce, and imprisoned in the same apartment with General Wadsworth. The latter thought this occurred about the middle of April, 1781. Burton says it was in March. From reports and hints which were deemed authentic, both parties believed that certainly the General, and probably the Major, were to be sent, in convenient time, either to Halifax or to New York, and thence to England, where they would be kept, and treated as prisoners during the war, the length and events of which were entirely uncertain.

They therefore soon formed a resolution neither to cross the Atlantic, nor to linger in protracted incarceration, and determined to escape, or perish in the attempt. They took a view of their geographical situation, with which both, and particularly the General, had previously been acquainted. Bagaduce they knew was a peninsula, a mile and a half in length from north-east to south-west, and about a mile in mean breadth, surrounded on all sides by water, except at its northerly part, where two coves from the east and west approximate each other within one hundred rods or less, having an isthmus or marsh by which the peninsula is joined to the mainland. The bed of the northwestern cove, and the beach of the Penobscot, contiguous, were sandy, and uncovered at low water, the height of the tides at that place being uniformly about fourteen feet. An escape was utterly impracticable unless effected in this quarter. The garrison was on crowning ground in the central part of the peninsula, between which and the isthmus, a distance of half a mile, were rocks, stumps and brush. In form the fort was tetragonal, with a bastion at each corner, constructed by an embankment twenty feet in height, exclusive of the exterior moat, guarded by pickets. The walls, which were secured by a friezing at the top, and chevaux-de-frieze at the bottom, were sufficiently capacious to contain a commodious block-house in the center of the area, containing apartments for officers and barracks for the soldiers. The prisoners' room was between two others severally occupied by the officers. One end of it was the wall of the building, the other formed in part the side partition of a long entry. From this the entrance was by a door containing a window sash, which was frequently opened by the guards. Without the fort, within upon the walls, and near the doors of the block-house, sentinels were posted, and also two in the entry near the prisoners' door. The gates were shut at sunset, and a picket guard was placed around the fort and towards the isthmus to prevent escape to the mainland.

From items of information acquired in reply to questions asked with apparent indifference, and from a refusal either to parole or exchange them, as had been formally proposed by Governor Hancock, the apprehension of the prisoners became strengthened into a belief that they were soon to be transported to some unknown destination. Hence, they justly inquired within themselves, "What are we to expect from such enemies, exasperated as they are by a war, expensive and hitherto inglorious to them, prosecuted too against men who are regarded as rebels? It is true, that if we fail in our attempt to escape, chains and dungeons await us; but then, at worst, our captivity, which is now grievous, will then only be galling." Thus wrought up to a desperation not to be expressed, and only equalled by the emergency, they formed their resolution with an unshaken firmness, and their plans with an ingenuity that nothing but the event itself could pronounce either wise or foolish, while the undertaking was exceedingly daring, if not highly presumptuous.

As their room was ceiled overhead with pine boards, they finally determined upon this plan of escape: To cut off one of these boards, and

[16]

thus open an aperture sufficiently large for a man to pass through, to ascend by it, thence proceed along the joists over the officers' apartments, and lower themselves down silently into the entry, by means of a blanket, thence pass directly across the intervening space and up the embankment, where from their windows they had seen a travelled path; and thence by further aid of their blankets slide down from the friezing into the ditch, and hasten to the beach at the westerly extremity of the isthmus, which at low water might be easily passed. They began upon the ceiling in the night with a penknife, but immediately found that the sound of their unskilfull cutting, made in the hours of silence and darkness, would assuredly betray them, as would their appearance in the daytime. Thus defeated, they were convinced that nothing could be done upon the ceiling except by daylight, nor was there more than an hour of that time, between twelve and one of the clock, while the officers were dining, that the work could be prosecuted, so frequently were they visited and viewed by their sentinels through the sash door.

Next they obtained from Barnabas Cunningham, their waiter, a gimlet, for which Major Burton made him a present of a dollar, pretending it as a reward for his courtesy, rather than a price for the article. This, by their care, excited no suspicion, and even if it had been otherwise, they knew the waiter would never make a disclosure which might give himself trouble. They began to use the gimlet as soon as and often as they dared, but the work went on slowly. Wadsworth, a man of middle stature, when standing on the floor could only reach the ceiling with the ends of his fingers. But Burton, whose height was about six feet and a half, could use the instrument without a chair. The work therefore devolved almost entirely upon him. It was important to make the most of their hour, and of the period when the garrison was under arms on parade. At those times therefore the waiters were purposely sent away on errands and the prisoners commenced walking in their room, corresponding with the steps of the sentinel marching through the entry, all passing by the glass door together. It was soon ascertained that, by a comparative adjustment of steps and a mutual measurement of time and distance, the passage of their guards through the entry occupied twice as long as it did themselves to pace across their room. Therefore as soon as the prisoners and sentinels at the same moment passed the door in the same direction, Burton stopped short, turned his gimlet quickly, then withdrawing it, joined Wadsworth in his second turn, he having continued his walk with a little heavier step than when alone, to give the sound of two persons walking. Thus the work was pursued from day to day, every perforation being filled with a paste composed of bread and butter. In three weeks the board was riddled with holes twice across, and the interstices cut, leaving only a few grains of wood at the corners to hold the piece in place. As Burton worked, his companion brushed into the fireplace with a handkerchief any chips or dust that fell upon the floor.

To prepare for their anticipated escape, they reserved from their meals bread and meat, which they dried. They made from their firewood pretty large skewers, purposing to fasten the corners of their blankets to the stakes in the friezing at the top of the wall, and thus let themselves down the exterior embankment of the fort. Being now ready for their departure, every day and incident increased their anxiety. As the officers and other visitors were often gazing around the room, it was feared that the discoloration of the bread by the butter, which composed the paste that filled the perforations, would betray them. In fact, some expressions had been dropped by officers, which to the ever jealous minds of the prisoners led to a suspicion that their design was known. They were also alarmed by a report that the privateer, which was to carry them away, was daily expected. Thus a long week elapsed, without a single night favorable for their escape, as they desired one which was dark and stormy.

At length, on the evening of June 18, 1781, a violent tempest occurred, attended with profound darkness, intermitted with flashes of vivid lightning. At about eleven o'clock the lightning ceased, and the rain began to fall in torrents. The opportunity which they had so anxiously desired, they believed had arrived. They went immediately to bed, and extinguished their candles while the sentinel was looking through the sash door. In a short time both arose and dressed themselves. At first Wadsworth in a chair, and then Burton on his feet, labored with the penknife, until in about half an hour they had cut out and removed the perforated board. Burton, the larger of the two, ascended through the opening with considerable difficulty. Wadsworth followed, but they saw each other no more during that fearful night. Burton crept silently along the joists over the officers' heads, let himself down into the entry, and thence proceeding through the square, ascended to the friezing on the top of the wall. While lying there and waiting for the General, he heard the voice

[18]

of command at the opposite guardhouse, "Relief, turn out!"

Supposing by this that his companion was detected, he immediately threw himself over the friezing, and seizing it fast with his hands gave his body a pendulous swing, then gently loosing his hold, struck with his feet the chevaux-de-frieze unhurt. To avoid the sentry-boxes he proceeded down the hill over rocks to the Penobscot at the northwesterly part of the peninsula, as previously proposed, "where the Americans landed in their first attack upon the British, two years before." As it was now of the utmost importance to elude any search and pursuit which might be made, and although in his anxiety he had struck the beach too far down to the westward, he yet waded forthwith into the water, which in crossing the cove was up to his chin. Much deluded, feeling his way in the dark, and sometimes swimming, he did not reach the opposite shore until daybreak. He then travelled a mile or more along the eastern margin of the river. At less distance than two gunshots he saw the enemy's barges, but which evidently had made no discovery. The rain had ceased, the opening morning was fair, and at sunrise he was safe on the bank of the river, perhaps seven or eight miles from the fort. His cup of happiness would have been full, had the General, whom he supposed retaken or drowned, been with him. While thus ruminating, he saw his fellow-prisoner calmly seated beside a canoe. The joy of their meeting can be easily imagined.

Crossing the river in the canoe, they landed at Sandy Point opposite, near the south end of Orphans' Island. They then shaped their course through the woods towards Belfast, and crossing the river Passagassawakeag in a boat found there, took refreshments at the house of Mr. Miller, where the village now is. Through fear of seizure by the villainous tories, and of recapture by the British, they did not dare to stay over night in the house, but went a mile into the woods and lodged on the ground. The next morning they pursued their way to Canaan (now Lincolnville) then a plantation of three families, thence to Warren, and on the third day reached Burton's residence in Cushing.

Burton knew that the treacherous tories, if they heard of his arrival, would devise some scheme to retake him. He therefore remained at home only a single night, and then went to Boston. Not finding any vacancy in the army which he wished to fill, he took a commission of Captain of Marines on board of a twenty-gun ship, commanded by Captain Thomas Dinsmore. After cruising for about a month near Newfoundland, the

vessel's course was shaped for Cape Clear, off Ireland, intending to inter-
cept a fleet of merchantmen from the West Indies. In October, 1781,
seeing four ships at the windward which they supposed were a part of the
fleet, they stood for them. To their surprise they were found to be three
British frigates and a sloop of war. Our ship, unable to escape, the wind
blowing a gale, was taken, and her crew imprisoned in the castle of Cape
Clear until the following February, after news had arrived of the surrender of Cornwallis. They were then removed to England, and confined in the old Dunkirk seventy-four, from which the overtures of peace
set them at liberty. In an enemy's land, without money and without
friends able to assist him, Major Burton succeeded in getting a passage to
L'Orient, in France, and thence in the frigate Alliance, Captain Harden,
was brought to the shores of his beloved country, and landed at New Lon-
don, in Connecticut. From that place, with only eight shillings in money,
he accomplished a journey home, two hundred and sixty miles, before the
end of May.

When the privations and perils of war were over, Burton with many
thousands, like the worthy Cincinnatus, returned to the plough, to enjoy
in straitened circumstances, and yet with a cheerful spirit, liberties and
privileges, no less the bounties of heaven because they were the price of
blood. Agriculture was his principal pursuit, although to some extent he
engaged in navigation. On the reorganization of the militia under the
statute of 1785, he was chosen lieutenant-colonel of the fourth regiment in
the eighth division, and subsequently had the command of it. He held his
commission until 1796, when he resigned. The next year he was the representative of Cushing in the General Court of Massachusetts. The first
representative from Cushing was his brother-in-law, Edward Killeran.
He was eight years a magistrate, and never filled an official position which
he did not honor. But in no sphere were his credentials more heartily and
justly awarded him, than by the Christian community. For more than
thirty years he was a devout professor of religion, and at the time of his
death was a deacon in the Baptist Church in Warren. He married
Hannah Church of Bristol, Rhode Island, before he quit the service there.
Two sons and four daughters survived him.

In person, Col. Burton was a large, tall and straight man, although in
his latter days a little bent forward. His complexion was light and
expressive, in motion and conversation he was quick and animated. In

mind he was discerning, ingenious and otherwise liberally endowed. He had a taste for mathematics and for military tactics, and especially for reading the scriptures and works upon history. Such was this worthy man, beloved by all his acquaintances, useful to his country, and happy in his death.

The following children were born to Col. Burton:

1. Benjamin, 3d, married a Jameson.

2. Thomas, 2d, born about 1784; married Lydia Young of Cushing, Jan. 10, 1813; resided in Warren village in the home later occupied by William H. Hodgman; and died Sept. 28, 1850.

3. John, 3d, married first, Mary Norton; second Rebecca Vaughn who died Sept. 10, 1865.

4. Elizabeth, born in 1787; died March 1, 1877; married first, Anselm Vaughan of Warren, Aug. 5, 1808; second, Deacon John Miller who was born Nov. 16, 1781; died June 1, 1857.

5. Hannah, married John L. Robinson of Cushing, Jan. 16, 1814. He resided for a short time in Union, but died in Searsmont.

6. Sarah, married Capt. Dunbar Henderson, July 18, 1815.

7. Ann, married first Capt. Robert Norton; second, Dr. Thomas D. Ralburn, May 17, 1830; resided in Newton, Mass.

Col. Burton's widow died Aug. 21, 1834.

BURTON, THOMAS. He enlisted March 5, 1776, as a private in Capt. Benjamin Plummer's company, stationed at St. Georges, and served until Sept. 6, 1776. He also served as corporal in Capt. Henry Sherburn's regiment. Mr. Burton's name appears on the Continental army pay accounts for service from April 1, 1778, to March 31, 1779, when he was reported discharged. His term of enlistment was for three years. He was first lieutenant in Major Benjamin Burton's volunteer company under Brig. Gen. Wadsworth, serving from April 20, 1781, to Nov. 20, 1781. He was also a member of Capt. Abijah Child's company, Col. John Greaton's 2d regiment, but the year of his service was not given in the muster return. Mr. Burton was the son of Capt. Benjamin Burton and a brother of Col. Benjamin Burton. He resided and died at Calais in 1837 or 1838. His first wife was Betsey Barter. His second wife was Susan

McCobb, a member of the McCobb family of Cushing. The mother of his children was probably the second wife. The children:

1. Edward, married and resided in Philadelphia.

2. Dorothy Y., married James H. Sanford; resided in Topsham and died in 1847. Her intentions of marriage were published Sept. 16, 1837.

3. Thomas, married Eliza Cunningham of Belfast; resided in New York.

4. Isaac, married Sarah Fish of Lincoln where he resided.

On September 25, 1855, the mother married Rev. James Farquharson of Williamsburg, N. Y. She died in Lincoln in March, 1872, Mr. Farquharson having died in February, 1858.

BURTON, WILLIAM. He enlisted as a private in Capt. Benjamin Plummer's company March 5, 1776, and served until Dec. 6, 1776, being stationed at St. Georges. He was a brother of Col. Benjamin Burton and grandson of Benjamin Burton who died on the passage from Ireland to St. Georges. He resided and died in Cushing, March, 1842. By his first wife, Jane Robinson, he had the following children:

1. Jane, died young.

2. Nancy, married Capt. Andrew Robinson; resided and died in St. George.

3. William, 2d, married first, Elizabeth Parsons of Cushing; second, Lucy Spear of Warren, daughter of Thomas Spear. She was born Oct. 23, 1794. He was killed in Warren, Jan. 2, 1821, by a falling tree.

4. Jane B., married John Montgomery of Townsend.

5. Isaac, married Nancy Parsons; resided in Cushing; died in Boston.

6. Matthew, born May 10, 1792; married Margaret Robinson of St. George, Oct. 29, 1818; resided in Rockland, and was a caulker by trade.

7. Eliza, died young.

8. Elizabeth, married Ephraim Robinson; resided in St. George. By his second wife, Chloe Bradford, he had the following children:

9. Sarah.

10. Chloe, died young.

11. Thomas, married first Rachel Vinal; second, Lucy (Vinal)

Burton; resided in Cushing.

12. Sarah.
13. James, married Lucy Vinal; resided and died in Cushing.
14. Chloe, died young.
15. Alfred, died young.
16. Elbridge, died young.
17. John R., married Lydia Bradford; resided and died in Cushing.
18. Lucy, died young.
19. William, 3d, married Miss Hyler; resided in Cushing and died in New Orleans.

CLARK, WILLIAM. It was ordered in Council, July 10, 1776, that a commission be issued to Mr. Clark as 2d lieutenant in Archibald McAllister's company, Col. William Jones' 3d Lincoln county regiment. He served two days in retaking and guarding the mast-ship "Gruell." On Sept. 15, 1777, he joined Capt. Joseph Jones' company and was on the march from June 29, 1779, to July 16, 1779, when he was discharged. Later he was a lieutenant, commanding a detachment, serving in Lincoln county from August 25, 1780, to Sept. 6, 1780. He also commanded a detachment under orders of Brig. Gen. Wadsworth from Sept. 22, 1780, to Oct. 24, 1780. After his discharge he enlisted as a private in Capt. Jordan Parker's company, Col. Samuel McCobb's regiment, July 8, 1781, and was discharged Dec. 1, 1781.

COOMBS, JOSEPH. He served as sergeant in Capt. Philip M. Ulmer's company, Col. Samuel McCobb's regiment, in the Penobscot expedition from July 8, 1779, to Sept. 24, 1779.

CROCKER, TIMOTHY. He served in Capt. Benjamin Plummer's company stationed at St. Georges for the defense of the sea coast, from February 4, 1776 to Dec. 10, 1776. He was a resident of St. George in 1790.

DAVIS, JOHN. He enlisted May 3, 1780 as a drummer in Capt. Jeremiah Goodwin's company, Col. Joseph Prime's regiment, under Brig. Gen. Wadsworth to the Eastward, the length of his service being six months and eighteen days. According to the muster roll for May, 1780, he served eight months from May 5, 1780, in the same company and regiment. Mr. Davis was a resident of St. George in 1790.

DYER, ANTHONY. He served as a private in Capt. John Blunt's

MAINE SOLDIERS AND SAILORS

company, Major William Lithgrow's detachment of militia, between Sept. 10, 1779, and Nov. 10, 1779, defending the frontiers of Lincoln county in the Penobscot region. Mr. Dyer's intentions of marriage to Hannah Heasey were filed with the town clerk of Cushing, August 20, 1789. His name appears as a resident of St. George according to the census of 1790.

FALLEY, FREDERICK. He enlisted June 10, 1775, from Westfield, Mass., in Capt. Warham Peak's company, Col. Donaldson's regiment. During service he received an order for a bounty coat or its equivalent in money dated Dec. 23, 1775 in camp at Roxbury, Mass. At the battle of Bunker Hill, Mr. Falley, then fourteen years of age, was the drummer for his father, Richard Falley, Jr., who commanded a company in that engagement, and drummed all through the fight. Later in the war Frederick Falley was promoted to the rank of major in recognition of his military services.

FALLEY, RICHARD, Jr. He served as ensign in Capt. Park's company, Col. Donaldson's regiment; also as lieutenant in the same company and regiment, in 1775. Later in the year a report was made by a committee appointed to consider the expediency of appointing him as an armorer, setting forth that he was a complete master of the business, recommending that he be employed in said capacity and be allowed 40 shillings per month in addition to his pay as ensign. He went to Boston with a company of seventy men on hearing of the battle of Lexington, April 19, 1775. He took part in the battle of Bunker Hill, June 17, 1775, and was a witness to the surrender of Gen. Burgoyne to Gen. Gates at Saratoga, October 17, 1777. In a list of officers dated 1776, his name appears as first lieutenant in Capt. Jedediah Southworth's company, Col. Lemuel Robinson's regiment. As first lieutenant, with other officers in Capt. Josiah Smith's company, he was granted beating orders by the Provincial Congress on April 11, 1776, for enlisting men to serve in a regiment to fortify the town and harbor of Boston. He was further granted beating orders for Hampshire county, Mass.

Mr. Falley was the son of Richard and Anna (Lamb) Falley, and was born in Cushing, Jan. 31, 1740; died in Westfield, Mass., Sept. 3, 1808. He married Margaret Hitchcock at Westfield, Dec. 24, 1761 or 1762. She was born May 25, 1741; died in Volney (now Fulton), New York, Feb. 11 or 18, 1820. At the age of sixteen he was a drummer in the

French and Indian war, and at the capture of Fort Edwards, on the Hudson, was made prisoner by the Indians, adopted by an Indian chief, taken to Montreal, and was finally bought by a woman for sixteen gallons of rum, and by her was sent home to Westfield.

He lived in the old Mt.Tekoa homestead in Westfield, and in a secluded ravine close by, unobserved by the British soldiers, he made the celebrated Falley muskets for the American army. One of the muskets, with "R. F." engraved on it, is still extant, and was presented to President Cleveland a few years before his death. The old foundations of the gun factory are still standing. Nearby is the site of the Falley glassworks. Mrs. Thomas B. Mosely of Westfield, a descendant of the Falleys, owns a solid glass rolling pin, a wine glass and goblet, all made in the Falley glass factory nearly 150 years ago.

The old gunmaker lies in the ancient moss-grown Mechanic street cemetery in Westfield, where Gen. William Shepard, another Revolutionary patriot, is buried. A few years ago a fund was raised to put the cemetery in repair, to which fund his great-granddaughter, Rose Elizabeth Cleveland, made a contribution. A few months before her death Miss Cleveland visited the Isle of Guernsey, seeking information concerning the Falley family. The name is Norman-French, and was originally spelled Faille, but later was corrupted to the present form of spelling. During her absence in Europe I wrote Miss Cleveland at her New York address for additional information concerning her family, but no reply was made to my communication. Lieutenant Falley was for many years superintendent of the armory at Springfield, Mass., and was noted as a man of powerful physique and great strength. One of his chief claims to fame is that he was the great-grandfather of President Cleveland. All his children were born either in Westfield or Springfield.

1. Louisa, born Dec. 3, 1763; married Medad Fowler; died May 20, 1807.

2. Frederick, born Jan. 2, 1765; died unmarried July 5, 1828, in Ohio. See preceding sketch.

3. Margaret, born Nov. 15, 1766; married Dea. William Cleveland, grandfather of Grover Cleveland; died Aug. 10, 1850, at Black Rock, near Buffalo, New York.

4. Richard, born Sept. 15, 1768; married Amanda Stanley; died Feb. 28, 1835, in Ohio.

5. Russell, born Oct. 5, 1770; married Pamelia Chapman of Blandford, Mass.; died March 29, 1842, in Perrysburg, Wood County, Ohio.

6. Daniel, born Dec. 3, 1772; died young.

7. Daniel, 2d, born Nov. 15, 1773; married Elizabeth Holland of Chester, Mass.; died in Fulton, N. Y. at the age of 80.

8. Ruth, born Dec. 7, 1775; married Samuel Allen; died in 1827 in New York City.

9. Lewis, born Jan. 15, 1778; died unmarried in 1810, at Charlestown, South Carolina.

10. Samuel, born Oct. 9, 1780; married Ruth Root of Montgomery, Mass.; died in 1873, in Granville, Ohio.

11. Alexander, born April 4, 1783; disappeared—not heard from after the age of 33 years.

FOSTER, JOHN. In a list of men returned to Col. David Cushing, dated at Weymouth, Mass., Jan. 2, 1778, the name of Mr. Foster appears among those who were selected to serve in the Continental army, drawn from the companies of Capt. Thomas Nash and Capt. Samuel Waldo. His residence at this time was given as St. Georges. Later he enlisted from the town of Weymouth for three years, joining Col. Benjamin Burton's company, being a part of the regiments of either Col. Sherburne or of Col. Crane. He first enlisted April 18, 1777, being attached to different commands until March 17, 1780 when he was discharged.

GARDNER, DANIEL. He enlisted as a private from the now town of St. George in the Penobscot Expedition in Capt. Philip M. Ulmer's company, Samuel McCobb's regiment, and served from July 8, 1779, to Sept. 24, 1779; also as lieutenant in Alexander Kalloch's company between Nov. 13, 1779, and Feb. 13, 1780. This company was detached from Col. Wheaton's and Col. Jones' regiments by order of Brig. Gen. Cushing to protect the eastern part of Lincoln county, and was stationed at Camden and St. Georges.

GAY, ELEAZER. He served as a private in Capt. Benjamin Plummer's company from Sept. 5, 1776, to the date of his discharge, Dec. 10,

OF THE REVOLUTIONARY WAR

1776. The company was stationed at St. Georges for defense of the sea coast.

Eleazer Gay, with his two brothers, Wellington and Jonah, came presumably from Attleboro, Mass., Eleazer settling on Gay Island, Cushing, Wellington at Friendship and Jonah at Union. He came to Cushing about 1785 as in that year Robert Robinson conveyed to him all his interest in Burton, now Gay, Island. This conveyance was followed by one made by Nathaniel Bartlett conveying his interest therein. In 1797, Gay purchased of Isaac Jameson his interest in the island, paying $200 therefor. Jameson acquired title thereto from Paul Jameson, his several predecessors in title claiming under the above-named Nathaniel Bartlett. The fact that on the 29th of August, 1814, Israel Thorndike, David Sears and William Prescott, of Boston, conveyed to Gay by warranty deed the whole island would necessarily lead to the conclusion that the former alleged owners had no more than a squatter's title. By this deed Thorndike and Sears conveyed fourteen-sixteenths and Prescott two-sixteenths. The island was described as "being number twenty-two on the original plan of islands belonging to the Waldo Patent, and known by the name of Burton island, and contains one hundred and sixty-one acres, be the same more or less." June 29, 1819, Eleazer Gay conveyed his interest in the island, for the first time called Gay Island, to his sons, Eleazer Gay, Jr., and Mark Gay. The major part of the island is now owned by Harry A. Thompson of Lowell, Mass., the manufacturer of "Moxie."

Eleazer Gay married Jane Jameson, a daughter of Paul Jameson of Friendship. Mr. Gay was born Sept. 11, 1748; died Dec. 11, 1822. His wife was born March 1, 1756; died Nov. 14, 1818. Their children:

1. Elizabeth, born Nov. 4, 1775; died April 15, 1861; married Hatevil Libby of Warren.

2. Ann, born Feb. 15, 1778; died Feb. 15, 1869; married Alex. Allen of Cushing.

3. Sarah, born Nov. 17, 1780; died Feb. 23, 1788; never married.

4. Job, born May 15, 1783; died September 30, 1852; married Lowly (Jameson) Burton, widow of Benjamin Burton, 3d. He died Sept. 30, 1852.

5. Hannah, born April 1, 1786; died June 11, 1853; married Cor-

nelius Bradford of Friendship. Her son Allen Alexander Bradford represented Colorado in the 39th and 41st Congresses. He was appointed Judge of the Supreme Court of Colorado by President Lincoln, June 6, 1862.

6. Eleazer, Jr., born Sept. 12, 1788; died Sept. 8, 1831; married Elizabeth McIntyre. She died April 6, 1841.

7. Nancy, born April 16, 1791; died Jan. 22, 1873; married Darius Norton of Cushing.

8. Isaac J., born Dec. 29, 1793; died July 11, 1831; never married.

9. Robert, born June 1, 1797; died July 22, 1882; married Eliza B. Collamore of Friendship.

10. Mark, born June 2, 1800; died April 3, 1871; married, first, his cousin, Eleanor Jameson; second, Sarah (Watts) Giles, widow of Paul Giles. She was born April 2, 1795; died Nov. 1859.

GILLCHREST, SAMUEL. He was wounded in a skirmish at Harlem during Washington's retreat from New York, the British ball remaining in his side to the day of his death. As Mr. Gillchrest enlisted with the Rhode Island troops his military record will be found in that State. He married Hannah Robinson of Cushing, a daughter of Joseph Robinson. When he came to Maine he settled in St. George where he continued to reside until his death. On Jan. 29, 1785, he sold to George Gillchrest, probably a brother, a lot of land containing 104 acres, being a part of the neck of land situated on the east side of St. Georges river at Cutler's cove, and adjacent to land of Samuel Watts. He was the father of eleven children:

1. Capt. John, married Margaret Fogerty, Jan. 30, 1800; resided in St. George.

2. William, born Aug. 1780; married Betsey Norwood; resided in Montville and died in 1860.

3. Capt. Joseph, born in Cushing, May 20, 1782; married Sarah Carney, Jan. 6, 1803. She was born in Thomaston, at Beech Woods, November, 1780. Her parents, Thomas and Nellie (O'Murphy) Carney, Jan. 6, 1803. She was born in Thomaston, at Beech Woods, on farm No. 43, before 1760, where they continued to reside until their

death. The log house occupied by the Carney family was built on a gradual elevation within a few rods from the river bank. Husband and wife are buried a short distance south of the cellar which is still in existence. Their graves are marked by flat field rock. The Carney farm is now owned by Rev. Frank W. Wheelock, a Massachusetts summer resident. It was formerly owned by the late Elijah Norton, grandson of Dea. Elijah Norton. Capt. Gillchrest moved to Thomaston, Aug. 15, 1823 or '24. He became a wealthy, retired mariner, and died Sept. 7, 1864. In the State election of 1832 he was elected a Representative to the Legislature from Cushing. On Sept. 13, 1839, Capt. Gillchrest conveyed to John Stone of Burnt Island, his homestead premises, containing 162 acres, situated at North Cushing. The farm is crossed by Stony brook, and adjoined farms of Joseph Robinson and Archibald Robinson.

4. Hugh, married first, Betsey Hall; second, Hannah Clemonds in Knox, Waldo County, where he removed and married a third time.

5. Samuel, 2d, married Lydia Smalley; resided in St. George.

6. Archibald, died young.

7. James, married Deborah Robinson, daughter of Hanse Robinson, 2d.

8. Alexander, married first, Margaret Hyler; second, Mary McKeller, daughter of Archibald, and granddaughter of John and Martha (McCarter) McKellar of St. George. Mr. Gillchrest resided in St. George and died there Aug. 8, 1844.

9. Robert, married Betsy Hall; resided in St. George.

10. Sarah, married James Linekin, resided in St. George in the first house from the South Thomaston line.

11. George, married Margaret Linekin, resided in St. George.

GRAFFAM, PIERCE. His name appears on the army roll dated at Pownalborough, Aug. 20, 1778, of the men raised in Lincoln County to march to Providence to reinforce the regiments of Col. Wade and Col. Jacobs as returned by Brig. Gen. Cushing. He enlisted Aug. 3, 1778, from Col. Wheaton's 4th Lincoln County regiment. At the time of his enlistment he resided on the eastern side of St. Georges river, now St. George.

[29]

GRANT, EDWARD. He enlisted as a private in Capt. Samuel Gregg's company, Col. James Cargill's regiment, Aug. 25, 1775, and was discharged Dec. 31, 1775. The company was raised in St. Georges, Waldoboro and Camden and stationed in those towns for the defense of the sea coast. Mr. Grant was later a corporal in Capt. Bancroft's company, and according to the Continental army pay accounts he served from Feb. 6, 1777, to Dec. 31, 1799. He was also a member of Capt. Wiley's company, Col. Jackson's regiment, enlisting at Providence, R. I., Jan. 1, 1777, during the continuance of the war, but the army record does not give the year of enlistment or term of service. In the Continental army pay accounts he is credited as a member of Capt. Pierce's company, Col. Michael Jameson's regiment, from Jan. 1, 1780, to Dec. 31, 1780. In a descriptive list of the members of Capt. Pierce's 6th company, Col. Michael Jackson's 8th regiment, Mr. Grant's rank is given as sergeant; age, 21 years; stature, five feet and ten inches; complexion, light; hair brown; occupation, yeoman; birthplace and residence, St. Georges.

HALL, ISAAC. He was a member of Capt. Archibald McAllister's company, Col. William Jones' regiment, serving two days retaking and guarding the mastship "Gruell," his name appearing on the roll call dated at New Castle, Sept. 15, 1777. He enlisted in Capt. Archibald McAllister's company, Col. Samuel McCobb's regiment, and served from July 11, 1779, to Sept. 24, 1779, on an expedition to Majorbagaduce.

HALL, ISAAC. He enlisted as a private in Capt. Nathaniel Larrabee's company, July 9, 1775. He also served as a private in Capt. Richard Mayberry's company, Col. Ebenezer Frances' regiment, at Dorchester Heights in 1776. He served as corporal at North River, N. Y., May 30, 1778, and was discharged Jan. 29, 1779. He also served in Capt. Thomas Starrett's detachment from Col. Mason Wheaton's regiment, at Clam Cove, from June 28 to July 5, 1779. In the expedition against Castine he was first lieutenant in Capt. Nehemiah Curtis' company, Col. Jonathan Mitchell's regiment, serving from July 7, 1779 to Sept. 25, 1779 according to the pay roll on file in the Massachusetts archives.

Lieut. Hall was born about 1725, and was probably the son of Isaac and Abigail Hall of Harpswell. He married Joanna Coombs of New Meadows, and was probably the first ferryman at Sebascodegan island. He was a soldier in the French and Indian war and was at the taking of

Louisburg. He resided a time in old Thomaston, and then settled in St. George, where he died. He was the father of the following children:

1. Caleb, married Hannah Snow; resided in St. George, and died Feb. 1814.

2. Rev. Isaac, 2d, married Sarah Sayword; had charge of the Baptist Church in Knox, Waldo County.

3. Rev. Ephraim, married Polly Snow; was for many years the Baptist minister in St. George, and died Oct. 5, 1809.

4. Dea. Peter, married Polly Pierson; resided and died in St. George.

5. Lewis, born Feb. 28, 1765; married Anna or Hannah Dyer; resided in South Thomaston, and died Nov. 4, 1845.

6. Elijah, married first, Betsy Robinson; second, Rebecca (Mann) Coombs; intentions of marriage filed May 1, 1828; resided and died in St. George.

7. Mehitable, married a Stover; resided and died in St. George.

8. Joanna, married John Curtis; resided and died in St. George.

HALL, ISAAC (also given as Israel). He served as a private in Capt. Joseph Jones' detachment of militia from June 29, 1779, to July 16, 1779, at Camden, by order of Col. William Jones.

HALL, JAMES. He enlisted as a private in Capt. Benjamin Plummer's company, March 5, 1776 and served until Sept. 6, 1776. The company was stationed at St. Georges for the defense of the sea coast. On July 11, 1779 he enlisted as a private in Capt. Archibald McAllister's company, Col. Samuel McCobb's regiment, and served until Sept. 24, 1779, on an expedition against Majorbagaduce.

HALL, JOHN. He served as a private in Lieut. Alexander Kelloch's company twelve days between Nov. 13, 1779, and Feb. 13, 1780. The company was detached from the regiments of Col. Wheaton and Col. Jones by order of Brig. Gen. Cushing to protect the eastern part of Lincoln county, and was stationed at Camden and St. Georges.

HALL, OLIVER. He served one month and three days in Capt. John Blunt's company, Col. Samuel McCobb's regiment, between June 28, 1779, and Sept. 28, 1779, on the Penobscot expedition. He was allowed mileage for 120 miles from and to his home at St. Georges.

HANDLEY, JOHN. He enlisted as a private in Capt. John Parker's company, Col. Samuel McCobb's regiment, May 12, 1781, and was discharged Dec. 1, 1781, having served at the Eastward. The roll call was sworn to at Georgetown. He also enlisted in Capt. George Ulmer's company, Col. James Hunter's regiment, June 8, 1782. The company was raised for the defense of Eastern Massachusetts. He also served as a private in Capt. Thomas Starrett's detachment from Col. Mason Wheaton's regiment at Clam Cove, Rockport, from June 28, 1779, to July 5, 1779.

Mr. Handley was a native of Holland, while his wife, Lucy Lewis, was a native of Wales. She was probably a granddaughter of Yarley Lewis who was born in Wales about 1690 and was one of the early settlers in Cushing. Mr. Handley resided at times at Georges Fort in Thomaston, and in Canton, Mass. Their children:

1. Henry, killed by the Indians in 1756.

2. Joseph, killed at the same time as his brother.

3. Hannah.

4. William, resided and died in Roxbury, Mass.

5. Samuel, lost at sea.

6. Nancy, married Simeon Hyler of Cushing.

7. Lucy, married a Hathorn of Bangor; was drowned by the upsetting of a sail-boat in mouth of St. Georges river, when coming to St. George on a visit.

8. Jane, married John Whipple of Boston.

9. John, married Mary Etheredge; took up lots No. 29 and 30 of Middle Neck, in upper part of St. George where he resided and died. He was a mason by trade, having done mason work on the Knox mansion.

The late Elijah H. Handley of Rockland was a grandson of the soldier John Handley.

HART, THOMAS. He served as a private in Capt. Benjamin Lemont's company, Samuel McCobb's regiment, on the Penobscot expedition from July 9, 1779, to Sept. 24, 1779, when he was discharged from service.

HATHORN, SAMUEL. He enlisted as a private in Capt. Archibald McAllister's company, Col. Joseph Prime's regiment, April 24, 1780, and served under General Wadsworth at the Eastward until his discharge Dec. 3, 1780.

On January 26, 1743, Samuel Waldo conveyed to Samuel Hathorn lot No. 59, to William Hathorn lot No. 60 and to Alexander Hathorn lot No. 61, each lot to contain 100 acres, situated on the western side of St. Georges river, at what is now known as Hathorn's Point. It has been claimed by some that Samuel and Alexander were the sons of William, and by others that the three were brothers. Whether the Samuel who saw military service was he who came to Cushing in 1743, or another Samuel, a son of Alexander by that name, has never been definitely settled. The later Samuel married Elizabeth Tewksbury of Salem, Mass. His son, Aaron, grandfather of Alphonso Hathorn of Thomaston, was a representative to the legislature from Cushing in 1838 and 1841.

HATHORN, WILLIAM. He enlisted as a private in Lieut. Nathaniel Tibbett's detachment Sept. 8, 1779, and was discharged Nov. 1, 1779, serving at Penobscot. The detachment was raised to serve with guards on the sea coast in Lincoln County under Major William Lithgow.

The above named William Hathorn was probably a grandson of the William who came from Salem to Cushing in 1743. As there are many interesting facts connected with the history of the Hathorn family of more than local interest, they are herewith included in the military record of Samuel, the Revolutionary patriot.

Mr. Hathorn, 1st, executed his will in presence of Daniel Lewis, William Smith and Moses Robinson, Jr., Nov. 23, 1755, by which he gave to his son Alexander three pounds in lawful money and all his wearing apparel. The residue of his estate he gave to his widow Jean, and to his granddaughter Jean, who afterwards married Andrew Bird. The widow and granddaughter were appointed executors, but the former renounced executorship Feb. 24, 1764, and the latter March 6, 1764.

The family name was spelled Hathorn until Nathaniel Hawthorne, the author of "The Scarlet Letter," and our country's greatest prose writer, inserted the letter "w" and added the final "e." He changed the spelling of his name after leaving college. In 1630, Hawthorne's ancestor

William, at the age of 23, came from Wiltshire, England, with John Winthrop in the "Arbella," and settled in Dorchester, Mass. In 1636 he went to Salem which gave him large tracts of land to induce him to remove. He died in 1681. His son John was Chief Justice in the witch trials at Salem. John died in 1717. His son Joseph was a farmer. They were men who followed the sea. Joseph's son Daniel commanded a privateer, and Daniel's son Nathaniel was the father of the famous author of the same name.

When Dean Sills of Bowdoin College addressed the Baptist Men's League in Rockland, a few years ago, he incidentally referred to the late Gen. J. P. Cilley as being the son of a member of the famous class of 1825, of which the poet Longfellow and Nathaniel Hawthorne were members. He expressed surprise that upon examining the signatures of the entering class of 1825, soon after he assumed the presidency of Bowdoin College, he found that Hawthorne spelled his name Hathorn. Modesty on part of the writer of these sketches, who was present, forbade an explanation.

During the presidential campaign of 1852, Hawthorne wrote the official campaign biography of Franklin Pierce, of the class of 1824, the Democratic candidate for President. For this service, and his friendship for his college mate, Hawthorne was rewarded with the appointment to the Collectorship of the port of Salem. It was during his incumbency of the office that Capt. Nathaniel Hathorn of Cushing called on Collector Hawthorne for his vessel's clearance papers. The similarity of names caused Hawthorne to inquire into Capt. Hathorn's ancestry, and upon being informed that the Hathorns who settled in Cushing were born in Salem, it was soon discovered, upon a little investigation, that they were descended from William Hathorn, the immigrant ancestor.

HAWES, ROBERT. He was a member of Capt. Philip M. Ulmer's company, Col. Samuel McCobb's regiment, on the expedition against Castine, serving from July 8, 1779, to Sept. 24, 1779.

Mr. Hawes was living in the northern part of St. George in 1790, with one son, under sixteen years, and six women in the family. The first Robert of St. George is very hard to fit into the scheme of the Wrentham, Mass. Hawes family, where logically he belongs, because of the coming of Mathias and Abijah Hawes to the St. Georges river settlements. The best solution seems to be that Robert was the hypothetical son (probably named Robert) of Hezekiah and Esther (Ware) Hawes. If so, his father was born between 1723 and 1729, when there were no children registered in Wrentham of Hezekiah and Esther. They may have been somewhere else during these years, and some one may discover the missing link. Hezekiah and Esther had several children before 1723 and after 1729. The Ware genealogy gives her line very satisfactorily. Hezekiah Hawes was the son of Daniel Hawes, 2d, and Abial (altered to Nancy) Gay, and grandson of Edward Hawes, 1st, and Eleanor Lombard of Dedham, daughter of Thomas and Joyce Lombard. Abial, or Nancy, Gay was the daughter of John Gay and Mrs. Joanna Baldwicke. The dates are easily found in the Savage, Dedham and Wrentham records. Capt. Robert Hawes, son of Robert, 1st, married Lydia Kelloch, June 10, 1802. He resided in Rockland following his marriage.

HENDERSON, ROBERT. In the list of men belonging to the several transports employed on the expedition against Castine, according to the roll made up agreeably to a resolve dated March 23, 1784, and attested by Joshua Davis, agent, Mr. Henderson was reported as belonging to the sloop "Industry." Mr. Henderson was the grandson of Capt. Thomas Henderson who had charge of the block house at Pleasant Point in the war of 1744. Capt. Henderson was born in 1693 and died in Cushing, Sept. 25, 1755. He married the widow of the celebrated David Dunbar, surveyor of the King's woods, and governor of the territory of Sagadahoc.

Robert Henderson married Jane Young and resided for a time at Pleasant Point. He was at St. Domingo at the time of its great conflagration, and, after years of adventure, was drowned near home on a fishing excursion in 1812. On August 8, 1802, he sold his farm at Broad Cove to his brother-in-law, Deacon Elijah Norton. In his old age Mr. Norton sold this farm to his son Darius Norton, who in turn conveyed it to his son-in-law, Samuel Payson. The following children were born to Robert and Jane (Young) Henderson:

1. James, killed at sea by accident.

2. Capt. Dunbar, 2d, married Sarah Burton, July 18, 1815; resided in Thomaston and died at sea, July 10, 1829, off the Tortugas, in his ship William and John, bound to Europe.

[35]

3. Capt. William, 2d, married Lucy Vose, Jan. 30, 1815; resided in Thomaston and died Aug. 31, 1827. He was a twin to Capt. Dunbar.

4. Elizabeth, born about 1794; married first, Capt. Bartholmew Killeran of Cushing, Nov. 15, 1814; second, Samuel Allen of Thomaston, September 29, 1825. She died Dec. 5, 1851.

HILT, PETER. He enlisted as a private in Capt. Benjamin Plummer's company, March 5, 1776, and served until Sept. 6, 1776. The company was stationed at St. Georges for defense of the sea coast. He was later a member of Capt. Nicholas Crosting's company, Col. Samuel McCobb's regiment, from July 22, 1777, to Sept. 4, 1777. The certificate on the army roll sworn to at Penobscot, states that the company was raised for an expedition against St. John's river, Nova Scotia, for the term of six months, and was ready to enter on said service until date of discharge, Sept. 4, 1777. Mr. Hilt served as a corporal in Capt. Jacob Ludwig's company, enlisting Oct. 7, 1777, and was discharged Dec. 22, 1777. For this service he was allowed mileage for two hundred miles from St. John to his home in St. George. The company was raised for the defense of Machias, the roll being sworn to at Waldoboro.

HINDS, SAMUEL. He served as a private in Capt. Benjamin Plummer's company stationed at St. Georges for the defense of the sea coast from Feb. 4, 1776, to Dec. 10, 1776. Later he served ninety-four months and five days in Capt. Patten's Company, Col. Crane's regiment. Mr. Hinds was a resident of St. George and is buried in the cemetery at Wiley's Corner. He was a Revolutionary pensioner.

HOWARD, ANDREW. He enlisted as a private in Capt. Archibald McAllister's company, Col. Samuel McCobb's regiment, and served from July 11, 1779, to Sept. 24, 1779, in an expedition against Majorbagaduce, the roll being endorsed "Regt. at Penobscot."

HOWARD, JOSHUA. He served as sergeant in Capt. Philip M. Ulmer's company, Col. Samuel McCobb's regiment, from July 8, 1779, to Sept. 24, 1779, on the Penobscot expedition. He also served as 2d Lieutenant in Capt. George Ulmer's company, Col. James Hunter's regiment from March 20, 1782, to Nov. 20, 1783, when he was discharged. The company was raised for the defense of Eastern Massachusetts.

HUTCHINS, BENJAMIN. He served as a private in Lieut. Alexander Kelloch's company from Nov. 13, 1779, to Feb. 13, 1780, the com-

6666

pany being detached from the regiments of Col. Wheaton and Col. Jones by order of Brig. Gen. Cushing to protect the eastern part of Lincoln county and was stationed at Camden and St. Georges.

Mr. Hutchins was probably a son of Robert Hutchins who resided in Cushing prior to 1760. Inquiry and investigation have failed to reveal any facts concerning Robert Hutchins, except that he had at least two children, Sarah and Susan. Sarah married Archibald Robinson, 2d, son of Joseph Robinson and grandson of Dr. Moses Robinson who bought lot No. 22 of Gen. Samuel Waldo, Jan. 6, 1743. Their intentions of marriage were filed with Robert McIntyre, town clerk, Aug. 20, 1789. Susan married Jacob Ludwig in 1797. He died Nov. 5, 1858. Mrs. Ludwig died Feb. 24, 1838. Eleven children were born of this marriage. Dr. Moses Robinson Ludwig, the second child, resided in Thomaston and was one of the most noted physicians in Knox county in his day and generation.

HYLER (HILER) JACOB. He was employed as carpenter on the sloop "Machias Liberty," commanded by Capt. Jeremiah O'Brien of Machias, serving from Feb. 1, 1776, to Oct. 15, 1776.

JAMESON, CHARLES. He enlisted as a private in Capt. Benjamin Plummer's company March 5, 1778, and served until Sept. 6, 1778. The company was stationed at St. Georges for defense of the sea coast. He was also a member of Capt. Philip M. Ulmer's company, Col. Samuel McCobb's regiment, serving from July 8, 1779, to Sept. 24, 1779, on the Penobscot expedition.

JAMESON, EBENEZER. He was a corporal in Capt. Philip M. Ulmer's company, Col. Samuel McCobb's regiment, serving from July 8, 1779, to Sept. 24, 1779.

JAMESON, JOSEPH. He enlisted as a private in Capt. Philip M. Ulmer's company, Col. Samuel McCobb's regiment, serving from July 8, 1779, to Sept. 24, 1779, on the Penobscot Expedition.

JAMESON, PAUL, 2d. He served as a private in Capt. Philip M. Ulmer's company, Col. Samuel McCobb's regiment, from July 8, 1779, to Sept. 24, 1779, on the expedition against Castine. Mr. Jameson was the son of Paul Jameson, 1st, and was a seaman by occupation. He married Sarah Parsons, daughter of Lawrence Parsons of Broad Cove, Cushing, and resided on Burton or Gay Island. He died July 21, 1795, at the age of 34 years, and is buried in the Pleasant Point cemetery.

JAMESON, ROBERT. Served as 2d lieutenant in Capt. Cornelius Bradford's 6th company, 4th Lincoln county regiment of Massachusetts militia, his appointment appearing in a list of officers chosen by the several companies in said regiment as returned by Col. Mason Wheaton and others dated at St. Georges, June 3, 1776. It was ordered in Council, July 3, 1776, that said officers be commissioned which was followed by a report that the several commissions were issued the same day.

JOHNSON, ANDREW. He was a gunner on the brig "Julius Caesar;" commanded by Capt. Nathaniel Bentley. In a descriptive list of officers and crew, sworn to at the Port of Falmouth, June 21, 1780, Mr. Johnson was described as being thirty-three years of age; five feet seven and one half inches in stature; and of light complexion. Mr. Johnson was evidently the Andrew Ring Johnson who came to Cushing from North Yarmouth, and married Margaret Adams, daughter of Capt. Richard Adams in 1768. On May 14, 1770, Mr. Johnson bought of Michael Ralley (now Rawley) a lot of land, containing 62 acres, bordering on Maple Juice cove, which he sold to William Young, April 14, 1772.

KELLOCH, DAVID, 3d. He enlisted as a private in Capt. Samuel Gregg's company, Col. James Cargill's regiment, Aug. 25, 1775, and was discharged Dec. 31, 1775. The company was raised in St. Georges, Waldoboro and Camden for the defense of the sea coast. He also served as a private in Capt. Abraham Hunt's company, Col. Joseph Vose's regiment, from Jan. 1, 1777, to Dec. 31, 1779. According to the muster roll he enlisted Jan. 16, 1777, for three years. On March 30, 1777, he was mustered in Capt. Hunt's company, Capt. Patterson's regiment. Mr. Kelloch served as a private in Lieut. Alexander Kelloch's company, which was stationed at Camden and St. Georges from Nov. 13, 1779, to Feb. 13, 1780. The company was detached from the regiments of Col. Wheaton and Col. Jones by order of Brig. Gen. Cushing to protect the eastern part of Lincoln county. As a corporal he served in Capt. George Ulmer's company, Col. James Hunter's corps, April 26, 1782, to Nov. 20, 1782. He was at Valley Forge as a member of Capt. Hunt's company, Joseph Vose's regiment. He served as a soldier under Gen. Gates in 1777. He was also a soldier in the war of 1812 against England. In his application for a pension he states: "I belonged to the town of Cushing, District of Maine in 1776 and in December of that year I enlisted in the army for one year under Col. Bond of Watertown, I think, and served the time for which I enlisted in said Reg. In 1777 I enlisted in the First Massachusetts Reg. commanded by Col. Joseph Vose for three years and served that time and was honorably discharged. My residence Mar. 17, 1835, was in Warren."

Mr. Kelloch's first wife was Betsey Love of Boston by whom he had the following children:

1. John, 3d, married Mary Stover of St. George, and resided in South Thomaston.

2. James, 2d, married Hannah Madden of St. George, Jan. 7, 1808; resided and died in Belfast or Waldo.

3. Jane, died young.

4. William, 2d, born about 1793; married, first, Susan Snow, Dec. 20, 1821; resided and died in St. George; second, Hannah Haskell, May 27, 1832, daughter of Francis Haskell, probably a native of Deer Isle, born 1789, died Nov. 28, 1845; third, Ann Maria Hayden, April 8, 1846; born Dec. 13, 1812. She was the daughter of Luther Hayden.

5. Rachel, married Adam Boyd, Jr., who resided in Rockland. His father lived in St. George and died there April 17, 1850 at the age of 84 years.

6. David, 4th, married Eleanor Kelloch, a daughter of Thomas Kelloch.

His second wife was Polly Ross Kelloch to whom he was married July 25, 1833. No children were born of this marriage. His first wife died May 21, 1826. At times he resided in Warren and St. George. He died January, 1846, aged 91 years, and is buried in the cemetery at Wiley's Corner, St. George. Mr. Kelloch was a pensioner, his name appearing on the published list of Revolutionary war soldiers receiving state bounty.

KELLOCH, JAMES. His name appears on the list of men mustered by Nathaniel Barber, muster master for Suffolk county, Mass., dated at Boston, March 30, 1777, as a member of Capt. Hunt's company, Gen. Patterson's regiment. He served as a private in Capt. Hunt's company,

Col. Joseph Vose's regiment, from Jan. 16, 1777, to Dec. 31, 1779, according to the Continental army pay accounts. On Jan. 16, 1777, he enlisted at Valley Forge for three years, and was with his company throughout the terrible winter of that memorable year. He is reported as a member of Capt. Green's company, Col. Joseph Vose's regiment, serving from Jan. 1, 1780, to Jan. 16, 1780. He served as corporal in Capt. Archibald's company, Col. Prime's regiment, under Gen. Wadsworth, to the Eastward, from April 24, 1780, to Dec. 21, 1780, when he was discharged.

Mr. Kelloch was the son of John Kelloch of St. George and Isabella Cunningham, who was a native of Arrowsic. Eaton, the local historian, in his History of Thomaston, South Thomaston and Rockland, states that he died in the Revolutionary war, yet the official records of the war give the date of his discharge Dec. 21, 1780. These records were not then printed and available to Eaton.

KELLOCH, JOHN, 1st. He was a sergeant in Col. Samuel Gregg's company, Col. James Cargill's regiment, and served from August 25, 1775, to Dec. 31, 1775. The company was raised in St. Georges, Waldoboro and Camden, and stationed there for defense of the seacoast. He was also a member of Capt. Nathaniel Fales' company of Coast Guards. Either he or his son, John 2d, was a private in Capt. Archibald McAllister's company, Col. Prime's regiment, under Gen. Wadsworth to the Eastward, from April 24, 1780, to Dec. 21, 1780. Mr. Kelloch married Isabella Cunningham of Arrowsic, a small island town in Sagadahoc county. He resided and died in St. George.

KELLOCH, MATTHEW. He served under Commodore Samuel Tucker in the navy of the Revolution. He also served in Capt. Samuel Gregg's company of Coast Guards from April, 1775, to Jan., 1776, and in the frigate Boston of the Continental navy from Feb. 17, 1779, to Dec. 1779. Mr. Kelloch removed from Thomaston to St. George where he died March 22, 1824, aged about 90 years. The pension list, however, gives the date of his death as one year later. He married Mary Robinson by whom he had the following children:

1. Margaret, died unmarried in St. George.

2. Finley, 3d, married; resided and died in Camden.

3. Moses, married first, Mehitable Hasey of New Meadows; second,

Lydia Sayward, daughter of Richard Sayward. She was born about 1774, and died about 1826.

4. Hanse, married Sally Phinney of St. George.

5. Polly, married Adam Boyd of Broad Bay; resided and died in St. George.

6. Katie, married David Boyd; resided and died in St. George.

7. Jane, married Capt. Thomas Kenney; resided and died in St. George.

8. Sarah, married Jacob Robinson; resided in South Thomaston and died in St. George, April 6, 1813. Intentions of marriage were filed Dec. 1, 1796. He was the 11th and last child of Major Hanse Robinson of Cushing.

KELLOCH, WILLIAM. He enlisted as a private in Capt. Archibald McAllister's company, Col. Samuel McCobb's regiment, in the expedition against Castine, and served from July 11, 1777, to Sept. 24, 1777. He re-enlisted in Capt. McAllister's company, Col. Prime's regiment, under Brig. Gen. Wadsworth at the Eastward, and served from April 26, 1780, to Dec. 21, 1780, when he was discharged. On Nov. 13, 1779, he joined Lieut. Alexander Kelloch's company, stationed at Camden and St. Georges, and served to Feb. 13, 1780.

KILLERAN, EDWARD. He was commissioned July 2, 1778, as 1st lieutenant in Capt. Isaac Wiley's 5th company, Col. Mason Wheaton's 4th Lincoln county regiment of Massachusetts, and served to the end of the war. He was twice captured and imprisoned by the British, the first time at Castine, and the last near the close of the war at Charlestown, South Carolina. On Aug. 30, 1813, his son Edward, as commander, and Henry Cobb, as lieutenant, were commissioned to engage in privateering in the brig Dash of Portland. The brig had a capacity of 220 tons and was owned by Seward Porter, merchant, William Porter, mariner, both of Portland, and Samuel Porter, merchant, of Freeport.

Mr. Killeran was born in Boston, Sept. 27, 1751, and died in Cushing, May 23, 1828. He came to Cushing while a young man, and was for several years engaged in teaching and surveying in which he was successful and proficient. He afterwards followed the sea for some time in command of vessels which were built and owned by Cushing parties in shipyards which have not heard the sound of a hammer for nearly a century. He was also prominent in town affairs and took an active part in the politics of his county and State. He was moderator of the annual town meetings for seventeen years, besides serving in that capacity for more than twenty-five special meetings. He served for thirty-two years as town treasurer; four years as a member of the school-committee; one year as town agent, and five years as constable and collector of taxes. He also held many minor town offices. During the second war with England he was appointed on the Committee of Safety, and on the Committee of Correspondence in 1815. He was a member of the Convention which framed the present constitution of Maine, and a senator from Lincoln County in 1821 and 1823. He was a member of the General Court of Massachusetts from Cushing in 1789, 1798, 1812, 1813, 1814 and 1819.

Mr. Killeran married Elizabeth Burton, a sister of Col. Benjamin Burton. She was born Sept. 18, 1752; died July 7, 1831. Eleven children were born of this marriage:

1. Benjamin, born Aug. 25, 1775; drowned in St. Georges river at Warren, May 27, 1814; married Mary Pendleton who died in Thomaston, June 4, 1852 aged 73 years.

2. Edward, Jr., born June 29, 1777; died in Boston, Oct. 25, 1846; buried in Portland; married Lucy Reed.

3. Nancy, born Sept. 10, 1779; died May 27, 1827; married John Hall who was drowned July 27, 1823.

4. Rebecca, born June 10, 1781; died June 18, 1804; buried in Meeting House lot.

5. Elizabeth, born Aug. 17, 1783; married William Malcolm, June 21, 1816. He died in 1874.

6. Bartholomew, born Feb. 27, 1786; died June 18, 1823; married Elizabeth Henderson, Nov. 15, 1814. She was born about 1794.

7. William, born Feb. 16, 1788; died Sept. 12, 1819; married Lydia Gay who died in Boston.

8. Sally, born Nov. 17, 1789; married James Parsons who died Sept. 23, 1819; intentions of marriage filed Nov. 22, 1818.

9. Thomas C., born Oct. 25, 1791; married first, Harriet, sister of

Marius H. Young, and Jane (Young) Davis; second, Lavinia, ninth child of Royal Grinnell of Union. She was born March 16, 1800; married first, Stephen Huse, Sept. 12, 1819, who died Feb. 15, 1834.

10. Arthur F., born Oct. 10, 1793; married Mary Norton, daughter of Deacon Elijah Norton, Feb. 12, 1818, by Edward Killeran, Esq.

11. Eliza B., born Nov. 1, 1795.

LAMB, JOSHUA. He enlisted as a private in Sergeant Thomas Knight's scouting party raised by order of Brig. Gen. Wadsworth to scout from head of St. Georges river to Belfast and Penobscot river, and served from Sept. 10, 1780, until Nov. 10, 1780, when he was discharged. The army roll was certified to at Falmouth.

In a "List of Settlers at St. Georges River," supposed to have been compiled by Capt. John North about 1760, are included names of Edward Lamb, senior, Edward Lamb, junior, and William Lamb. The name of Lamb does not appear in the census returns of Cushing in 1790. Richard Lamb is mentioned as a subscribing witness in a deed from Gen. Samuel Waldo to Thomas White dated Dec. 14, 1736, by which he conveyed to him lots 23 and 24, situated on the west side of St. Georges river in Cushing. On the same day Edward Lamb, a carpenter, purchased of Gen. Waldo lots 25 and 26. Samuel Lamb, a clothier, also on said Dec. 14, purchased lots 27 and 28 of Gen. Waldo. On Jan. 27, 1743, William Lamb purchased of Waldo lots 17 and 18. Mr. Lamb sold lot 17 to Andrew Malcolm, July 12, 1771, for forty pounds sterling. On the same day he sold lot 18 to Haunce Robinson for the same consideration. At the time the deed was executed, Mr. Lamb gave his residence as Falmouth, District of Maine.

Daniel Lamb, a soldier in the war of 1812, was living in Lincolnville, Maine, in 1861, at the age of 65 years. In 1790 a Richard Lamb was a resident of Canaan plantation, now the town of Lincolnville. The wife of Capt. John McIntyre who was born in 1724 was a Mrs. Lamb of Cushing. John Lermond of Warren married Elizabeth Lamb of Cushing, July 8, 1771. His son John married Agnes Bird of Cushing, Dec. 1, 1796.

Anne Lamb was the daughter of Richard Lamb of Comb, Ireland, who apparently died on his way to America. His will, made on shipboard August 12, 1736, was proved in Boston Probate Court, 1737. He left money and goods on board the ship with him, to his son Edward, "now in New England," also to William, Richard, Elizabeth, Anne, Eleanor and Rebecca Lamb, and to his daughter, Sarah Ferris, "now in Ireland." Elizabeth married a Howard before July 4, 1737. Anne Lamb who married Richard Falley, senior, was the great-great-grandmother of President Cleveland. Her daughter, Mary, born in Cushing, Feb. 20, 1744, married Zachariah Bush at Westfield, Mass., Nov. 29, 1764.

LEWIS, GEORGE. He enlisted as a private in Capt. Archibald McAllister's company, Col. Samuel McCobb's regiment, July 11, 1779, and served until Sept. 24, 1779, on an expedition against Majorbagaduce. The pay roll on file in the Massachusetts archives is endorsed: "Regt. at Penobscot."

George, Nathaniel and William Lewis were probably brothers and sons of Daniel Lewis who died in Cushing, May 28, 1794, in the 69th year of his age. Daniel Lewis was the son of Yarley Lewis who was born in Wales about 1680. He was married April 28, 1702. John Lewis, son of Daniel, was born Sept. 18, 1763, and died April 19, 1838. He married Agnes Young, Jan. 14, 1796, who died June 20, 1848. In the winter of 1743, Gen. Samuel Waldo entered into a written agreement with Daniel and Charles Lewis to convey to them two lots of land in Cushing, each containing 100 acres, but being unable to perform the conditions of the agreement the Lewis brothers surrendered the agreement to Waldo. On June 20, 1746, Waldo extended the performance of the agreement for twelve months.

On April 17, 1777, Mrs. Sarah James of Warren sold lot No. 35 to Daniel Lewis containing 100 acres, adjoining the lot Waldo sold Lewis on the south. This was probably the same lot which Jane Jameson of Falmouth, a mantua maker sold to Mrs. James of Meduncook, widow of William James, July 17, 1772. This lot was devised to Mrs. Jameson by her father, Samuel Jameson.

The following children were born to John and Agnes (Young) Lewis:

1. Margaret, born June 6, 1798; died Oct. 3, 1801.
2. George, born Sept. 24, 1800; died Oct. 6, 1801.
3. Eliza, born April 25, 1802.
4. John, born April 14, 1804.

OF THE REVOLUTIONARY WAR

5. Jane R., born Aug. 9, 1806; died Feb. 27, 1884; married William J. Bradford.

6. Mary.

7. Ann.

LEWIS, NATHANIEL. He enlisted as a private in Capt. Archibald McAllister's company, Col. Samuel McCobb's regiment, July 11, 1779, and served until Sept. 24, 1779, on an expedition against Majorbagaduce. The pay-roll on file in the Massachusetts archives is endorsed: "Regt. at Penobscot."

LEWIS, WILLIAM. He enlisted as a private in Capt. Archibald McAllister's company, Col. Samuel McCobb's regiment, July 11, 1779, and served until Sept. 24, 1779, on an expedition against Majorbagaduce. The pay-roll on file in the Massachusetts archives is endorsed: "Regt. at Penobscot."

LONG, JOSIAH. He enlisted as a fifer in Capt. John Reed's company, Col. Samuel McCobb's regiment, July 21, 1781, and was discharged Dec. 1, 1781. The company was raised for the defense of eastern Massachusetts, now the State of Maine.

MADDEN, JOHN. His name appears in the descriptive list of men serving in the Continental army, with the rank of sergeant, in Capt. John Burnam's Light Infantry company, Col. Jackson's 8th regiment. He is described as 22 years of age, five feet and ten inches in stature, dark eyes, dark complexion, and a seaman by occupation. He was native of Pemaquid, but at the time of his enlistment he resided on the eastern side of St. Georges river. Mr. Madden enlisted Feb. 2, 1777, under Capt. Wiley at Providence, Rhode Island, and was discharged from service June 10, 1783. In his application for a pension he states that he was at Valley Forge during the terrible winter of 1777 as a private in Capt. John Wiley's company, Col. Michael Jackson's Massachusetts Continental Line. On March 17, 1835, he was residing in Waldo plantation, but for 30 years prior thereto he had lived in Belfast, Greenfield and Waldo.

MADDING, JOHN. According to the Continental army pay accounts, he served as a private in Capt. John Wiley's company, Col. Michael Jackson's regiment, from Feb. 10, 1777, to Dec. 31, 1779. He gave St. Georges as his residence at the time of service. He served as

MAINE SOLDIERS AND SAILORS

corporal in Capt. Pierce's company, Capt. Jackson's regiment, from Jan. 1, 1780, to Dec. 31, 1780. He was reported as having served twenty-five months and twenty-one days as a private, fifteen months as a corporal, and six months as sergeant while in the army. It is quite evident that John Madden and John Madding were identical persons—a difference in spelling being the explanation.

MALCOLM, ALLEN. He enlisted as a private in Capt. Archibald McAllister's company, Col. James McCobb's regiment, July 11, 1779, and served until Sept. 24, 1779, on an expedition against Majorbagaduce.

MALCOLM, ANDREW. He enlisted as a private in Capt. Jacob Ludwig's company Oct. 7, 1777, and was discharged Dec. 20, 1777. The company was raised for the defense of Machias. The roll-call was sworn to at Waldoboro. He also enlisted in Capt. Thomas Starrett's company, Col. Mason Wheaton's regiment, June 28, 1779, and served at Camden, Eastern Department, until July 5, 1779.

MALCOLM, JOHN. He served in the Penobscot expedition as a private in Capt. Benjamin Lemont's company, Col. Samuel McCobb's regiment, from June 26, 1779, until Sept. 24, 1779, when he was discharged.

MARSHALL, SAMUEL. He served as a private in Capt. Philip M. Ulmer's company, Col. McCobb's regiment, from July 8, 1779, to Sept. 24, 1779, in the expedition against Castine.

MARTIN, MOSES. He enlisted as a private in Capt. Timothy Heald's company, Col. Samuel McCobb's regiment, June 30, 1779, and was discharged Sept. 25, 1779, serving on the Penobscot expedition.

MARTIN, SAMUEL. He served as a private at Penobscot in Capt. Benjamin Plummer's company from July 6, 1779, until Sept. 24, 1779. The company was detached from Col. Jones' regiment for service under Col. Samuel McCobb on the expedition against Majorbagaduce.

McCOBB, JAMES (also given as James McCobb, Jr). On July 1, 1776, according to the list of officers returned by Dummer Sewall and others, Mr. McCobb was commissioned captain of the 4th company, 1st Lincoln county regiment of the Massachusetts militia. He was also captain of the 4th company, Col. Samuel McCobb's Lincoln county regiment, as appears by the regiment returns made by Col. Sewall, dated at Georgetown, Nov. 19, 1779. Although Capt. McCobb gave Georgetown as his residence at the time he received his commission as captain, he probably took up his residence at the close of the war in the plantation of Lower St. Georges, as his name appears in the census of 1790 as residing on the eastern side of St. Georges river. He died May 14, 1834, at the age of 88 years, and is buried in the Pleasant Point cemetery.

McINTYRE, JOHN. He served as a private in Lieut. Alexander Kelloch's company, which was detached from Col. Wheaton's and Col. Jones' regiments by order of Brig. Gen. Cushing to protect the eastern part of Lincoln county, from Nov. 13, 1779, to Feb. 13, 1781. The company was stationed at Camden and St. Georges.

McINTYE, WILLIAM. He enlisted as a private in Capt. Thomas Starrett's detachment from Col. Mason Wheaton's regiment, June 28, 1779, and served at Camden, in the Eastern Department, until July 5, 1779.

McLELLAN, JOHN. He served as a private in Capt. Archibald McAllister's company, Col. Samuel McCobb's regiment, from July 16, 1779, to Sept. 24, 1779, on the expedition against Majorbagaduce.

McLELLAN, SAMUEL. He served as a private in Capt. Archibald McAllister's company, Col. William Jones' regiment, in retaking and guarding the mast ship "Gruell."

McLELLAN, WILLIAM. He enlisted as a private in Capt. Reed's Company, Col. Samuel McCobb's regiment, July 23, 1781, and was discharged Dec. 1, 1781. The company was raised for defense of the sea coast of Eastern Massachusetts. Mr. McLellan died on board a prison ship in the Revolutionary war. He was the son of Capt. George McLellan, who married Mary Webster of Portland. Capt. McLellan was a shipmaster and was lost at sea with his son George. It is possible that John, Samuel and William McLellan resided in Thomaston when they entered military service. Members of the McLellan family, however, resided in Cushing in the early history of the town.

NORTON, ELIJAH. He was a private in Capt. David Noble's company, Col. John Patterson's 26th regiment. He was born at Edgartown, Martha's Vineyard, Mass., and died in Cushing, May 19, 1838, at the age of 78 years, 11 months and 19 days, and is buried in the Central, or Norton, cemetery, Broad cove. He held the office of moderator in 1805; assessor 1806; selectman, 1808 and 1816; and clerk 1815.

Albert B. Norton, United States Navy, in his "Descendants and Ancestors of Charles Norton of Guilford, Connecticut," claims that Thomas Norton, who left England for Guilford in 1639, descended from Le Sr. de Norville, who went from France to England, September, 1066; and that he married into the family of Valois. In the ninth generation the name was permanently changed from Sr. de Norville to Norton. See sketch of Robert Henderson.

NUTTING, JONATHAN. He served as a private in Capt. Thomas Starrett's detachment from Col. Mason Wheaton's regiment at Clam Cove from June 28 to July 5, 1779. He also served in Capt. Philip M. Ulmer's company, Col. Samuel McCobb's regiment, from July 8 to Sept. 24, 1779, on the Penobscot expedition.

On November 17, 1771, Mr. Nutting purchased of Henry Handley of Boston, administrator de bonis non of the estate of Richard Falley, senior, lot No. 3 in Cushing, situated on the west side of St. Georges river. The great-grandfather of President Grover Cleveland, Richard Falley, junior, was born on this lot. The farm is now owned by William M. Hoffses of Portland.

Mr. Nutting was born August 10, 1735, but his place of birth is unknown. He was twice married, his first wife, Hepsibeth, being a daughter of Rev. Robert Rutherford, who lived on a farm in Cushing, situated on the east side of Hathorn's Point road. This farm is now owned and occupied as a summer home by William L. McNamara of Bangor. Four children were born of this marriage: 1, Silas who married Elizabeth Gardner, May 25, 1818; he resided in Cushing and died in the West Indies; 2, Jonathan, 2d; 3, George; 4, Barbara, married Jacob Hyler. His second wife was Mary Butler of Edgartown, Martha's Vine-yard. Their intentions of marriage were filed with the town clerk of Cushing, August 14, 1792. The first child born of this marriage was Ebenezer who was lost at sea in the schooner Hercules; 2, Hepsibeth, born May 5, 1799; married first, Capt. William Biscay, July 8, 1821. He resided in Thomaston, and died in Norfolk, Virginia, August 24, 1826 while in command of a vessel named "Tobacco Plant."

Capt. Biscay's father, also named William, was a Frenchman by birth and a house-joiner by trade. He first came to St. George, where he married Catherine Long. The second husband of Hepsibeth was Capt. Peter Miller who resided in Thomaston. She died November 9, 1861. Capt. Miller was born on the island of Bonholm, Denmark, his family name being Peterson. Leaving Europe he bought American protection and sailed under the name of John Harris, but was naturalized under the name of Peter Miller. His second wife was Elizabeth (Nutting) Lermond, widow of Albert G. Lermond of Warren and a sister of his first wife. 3, Thomas, lost at sea as mate of the Hercules. 4, Mary, married Joshua Jordan, a merchant of Thomaston, October 28, 1827. He died July 16, 1834. 5, Eliza, married Alden Robinson of Cushing, March 11, 1834. He was born February 1, 1801, and died July 30, 1853. 6, Edward. 7, Clement, died unmarried. 8, Freeman, who died March 13, 1843.

An interesting episode in the life of Mr. Nutting near the close of the war is related by Eaton in his history of Thomaston at page 149 of volume 1.

In 1780, Jonathan Nutting, late of Cushing, being taken by the British as one of the crew of the brig Ruby of Boston, bound to Martinique, was carried to Barbadoes and confined on board the prison-ship of about 500 tons, which, stripped of sails and rigging, was moored in the centre of St. Lucie harbor. Here, with several hundred French and American prisoners, they were four months confined between decks, in the hottest part of the season, allowed to come on deck for air during the day only, and furnished with a scanty allowance of provisions. On deck they were strongly guarded and watched, and at night the hatches closed upon them and barred. So great were their sufferings, that Nutting and ten other Americans, formed and adopted a bold plan of escape. They were surrounded by armed vessels, privateers, merchantmen, and at a short distance a twenty-gun ship; while, as further security, a Letter of Marque of 150 tons and mounting 14 guns, lay outside the rest toward the entrance of the harbor. The plan being matured and a dark and foggy night favoring it, they began by working on the compassion of the sentries who had occasionally allowed, contrary to orders, two or three at a time of the sick and suffering prisoners to come on deck a few moments during the night, and who, lulled by a sense of security, were unusually indulgent on this occasion, allowing the several divisions of the eleven plotters to come up at intervals without sufficiently attending to their return. Contriving in the darkness to conceal themselves behind water casks, they, by means of a rope, let themselves down through a port-hole on to the main chains, divested themselves of clothing, except Nutting, who kept his handkerchief around his neck in which he had concealed two guineas and two silver dollars; and all successively swam to the Letter of Marque more than a mile distant. Waiting as agreed upon at the bows of this vessel till all but two had appeared, they climbed up her cable, disarmed and secured the forward sentinel sitting on the windlass fast asleep, and levelled the other who was crying murder and summoning all hands on deck in such a manner that one of the eleven, a Virginian, became frightened, swam back to his prison, dressed himself, and reported to the prisoners that all but he were lost. So far from it, however, they had, ere this, secured the companion-way, the entrance to the forecastle, got possession of all arms, cut the cable, sailed out of the harbor under the guns of the fort without being hailed, and reached the capital of Martinique in safety, with the Stars and Stripes waving above the British colors. Here the prize was sold for 4006 crowns, dividing 400 apiece to each of the ten captors,—one having deserted, and the two that were missing coming on board before they left the harbor.

PACKARD, MICAH. He served as a private in Capt. Thomas Starrett's detachment from Col. Mason Wheaton's regiment serving from June 26, 1779 to July 5, 1779, at Camden in the Eastern Department. During the American Revolution the Committee of Safety met at the house of Micah Packard of which Mason Wheaton was chairman, and John Shibles, clerk.

Micah Packard, with his brother Benjamin, came from Bridgewater, Mass. to Cushing in 1764. They were carpenters by trade and were employed by Moses Copeland in erecting his mills. On April 15, 1759, Micah bought of John Palmer the western part of lots one and two, containing one hundred acres, and built a dwelling house thereon which is now used by Irving E. Spear, the owner of the farm, as a wood house, the dimensions being 18 by 46 feet. The house occupied by the late Isaac Spear, a native of Warren, was built in 1832 by Capt. John Robinson, to whom Marlborough Packard sold his farm in 1803, the year he moved to Union with his father Micah, who sold the Palmer farm to his son Marlborough in August, 1787. The farm which the Packards bought in Union continued to remain in four generations of the family, when it was sold to Maynard Hunt. A few years ago the Spear house was struck by lightning and burned. A few months thereafter a modern farm dwelling house was built on the same site by Irving E. Spear.

A description of the Robinson house was furnished me several years ago by the late E. Sanford Bucklin of SouthWarren, to whom I am indebted for many interesting accounts of the early families and history of the northern part of Cushing. The house was nine foot, cock-tenanted posted. The frame was hewn, the walls studded with square-edged boards nailed on horizontally and covered with shaved pine shingles. Wrought iron nails were used throughout the building. The best room was on the eastern end, warmed by a large fire-place, while in the kitchen was a large fire-place for heating and cooking, a very necessary adjunct to good house-keeping at that time. Kitchen supplies were stored on shelves painted red, and tradition tells us that the paint was made of skimmed milk and red ochre. In the western end was a bedroom and pantry, with stairs leading to the unfinished chamber from the pantry. Poles were nailed to the rafters which were used for the hanging of the autumn crop of Indian corn, to protect it from moisture and the ravenous appetite of rats.

Mr. Robinson dying intestate, his farm was inherited by his children, Sarah A. Catland, Mary A. Creighton and Eliza Robinson. The latter purchased the interest of her sisters therein, Oct. 22, 1856. Miss Robinson retained the title until June 4, 1868, when she sold the farm to Isaac Spear.

Marlborough Packard was a natural mathematician. He excelled in the solution of mathematical problems and in the use of mechanical tools. He could make anything from a boot-jack to a wagon wheel, from a window to a spinning wheel, and in the construction of the latter he was a past master. All spinning wheels in this locality having the letters "M. P." carved on the end of the body are the work of Mr. Packard.

Bertram E. Packard, State Commissioner of Education, is a direct descendant of Micah.

PAGE, WILLIAM. He served in Capt. Benjamin Plummer's company, stationed at St. Georges for the defense of the sea coast, from February 4, 1776, to December 10, 1776.

PAYSON, SAMUEL, 2d. He enlisted in Stoughton, Mass., as a private in Capt. Nathaniel Clapp's company, Col. Benjamin Howes' regiment, July 26, 1778, and was discharged Sept. 11, 1778, serving in Rhode Island under Brig. Gen. Glover. He re-enlisted July 4, 1780, and was discharged Dec. 8, 1780. At the time of enlistment he was described as 22 years of age, five feet and nine inches in height and of dark complexion.

That he was 22 years old when he enlisted is a manifest error, as he was born in 1761, and enlisted in 1778. His son, Samuel Payson, 3d, informed the writer several years ago that his father was but 17 years old when he enlisted in Capt. Clapp's company. His father, Samuel Payson, 1st, joined the Revolutionary army at the time of his son's enlistment, and thereafterwards was closely identified with the patriotic cause.

At the close of the war the elder Samuel moved with his family from Sharon to Warren, but after residing there a short time he moved to Hope, where he died and is buried. Samuel, 2d, was born in Stoughton, Mass., April 20, 1761; died in Cushing, Sept. 22, 1849, and is buried in the Norton burying ground at Broad Cove. At the close of the war Mr. Payson moved to Cushing where he married Margaret Lewis, a daughter of John Lewis, one of the most prominent citizens in the early history of the town. After the death of his wife, he married Sarah Rivers, widow of Isaac Robinson. She was born April 14, 1781, and was married to Mr. Payson, Dec. 1812. For his services as a Revolutionary soldier, he received from the Government a pension of twelve dollars per month. There is no evidence to prove, as has been asserted by some of his descendants, that Samuel Payson of Hope was identified with Quakerism, the nearest approach to it in his family being that of his second wife, Annie, who was a member of the Quaker Church.

RAWLEY, EDWARD. He enlisted as a private in Capt. Archibald McAllister's company, Lieut. Col. Joseph Prime's regiment, under Brig. Gen. Peleg Wadsworth, at the Eastward, serving from April 12, 1780, to Dec. 15, 1780, when he was discharged. The army roll certificate was signed at Thomaston. Mr. Rawley was the son of Michael Rawley who settled in Cushing prior to 1760. The father purchased lot No. 42, situated on the westerly side of St. Georges river, on which he lived several years. According to the census of 1790 father and son were residents of the now town of St. George.

RIVERS, ARCHIBALD. His name appears on the pay roll of the officers and crew of the ship "Protector," commanded by Capt. John Foster Williams. He engaged May 3, 1780 and was discharged Aug. 17, 1780. Mr. Rivers was a son of Joseph Rivers who came from the north of Ireland and settled in Cushing prior to 1760. He married Nancy Gardner of Boston. His father Joseph, and Margaret his wife, conveyed to Moses River, Feb. 2, 1796, his homestead premises, situated on the western side of St. Georges river, containing 130 acres. On Oct. 9, 1824, Archibald Rivers and others, presumably his brothers and sisters, conveyed to Nancy Rivers, widow, 50 acres of land lying between St. Georges river on the east and Maple Juice cove on the west. Mrs. Rivers remained in possession of this lot until March 15, 1825, when she sold it to Thomas and Archibald Rivers.

ROBINSON, ALEXANDER. He was a sergeant in Capt. Benjamin Lemont's company, Major Lithgrow's detachment, from Sept. 15, 1779 to Nov. 1, 1779, serving near the Penobscot coast. The company's receipts for muskets, etc, were given by Sergeant Robinson to Capt. Lemont at Camp Coxe's Head, under date of June 8, 1781. He re-enlisted as private in Capt. Lemont's company, Col. Samuel McCobb's regiment, May 10, 1781, and was discharged Dec. 1, 1781.

ROBINSON, ANDREW. He served as a private in Capt. Benjamin Plummer's company from March 5, 1776, to Sept. 6, 1776. The company was stationed at St. Georges for the defense of the sea coast. An order on Alexander Houghton, dated at St. Georges, July 2, 1788, signed by Mr. Robinson, was made payable to Capt. Robert Henderson for payment of wages at Majorbagaduce while on board the sloop Sally, commanded by Capt. John Reed.

ROBINSON, ARCHIBALD. He was 2d lieutenant in Capt. Paul Dodge's 1st company, Col. Jones' 3d Lincoln county regiment of Massachusetts militia. He was commissioned May 23, 1780. Mr. Robinson was born Jan. 31, 1737, the fifth child of Dr. Moses Robinson, and was the first white child born in Cushing. He married Margaret Watson, who was born August 22, 1743, and died Sept. 1, 1817. She was the daughter of William Watson who came from the north of Ireland and after residing in several places in Maine came to Thomaston, settling at Watson's point, where he died Sept. 21, 1768. Mr. Robinson died Feb. 25, 1820 and is buried on the ministerial lot. He was the father of ten children:

[53]

1. William, 2d, born Nov. 27, 1762, married Catherine Packard, Oct. 3, 1793; resided in Cushing and died there June 26, 1822. He was the father of Edward Robinson, who was the Whig candidate for governor in 1842, 1843 and 1844.

2. Mary, born Sept. 27, 1764, and died unmarried.

3. Elizabeth, born Aug. 17, 1766; married Dea. James Fisher; resided in Warren and died October 1849. He was born in Scotland in 1760, died March 29, 1837.

4. Margaret, born Aug. 17, 1768; married first, William Watson, 3d, born Oct. 23, 1769; died Oct. 16, 1802. Her second husband was John A. Roscoe, to whom she was married June 27, 1805. She died in Friendship in 1822.

5. James, born Sept. 25, 1770; married Rachel, daughter of Lieut. James Thompson of Cranberry Island (a Revolutionary soldier who died in Friendship, Dec. 1, 1837, aged 93 years). Capt. Robinson died March 11, 1831.

6. John H., born Jan. 11, 1773; married Jane Sumner of Warren, who was born in 1780, daughter of Hepestill Sumner. Capt. Robinson resided in Cushing and died July 4, 1848.

7. Sarah, born March 21, 1775, died May 3, 1803; married Josiah Keith of Thomaston who was born in 1771; died Oct. 23, 1814.

8. Lucy, born Oct. 8, 1777; married William W. French of Warren.

9. Nancy, born July 2, 1780; died Feb. 18, 1861.

10. Archibald, 3d, born Jan. 8, 1783; married, first, Elizabeth Vose; second, Mary Vose, born Sept. 26, 1785; published May 16, 1811. She died Jan. 2, 1854.

ROBINSON, HAUNCE. He enlisted as 2d lieutenant in Capt. Samuel Gregg's company, Col. James Cargill's regiment, from August 25, 1775, to December 31, 1775. The company was raised in St. Georges, Waldoboro and Camden and stationed there in defense of the sea coast. Official record of a ballot by the House of Representatives dated January 30, 1776, for field officers of the several regiments raised in Lincoln county, shows that he was chosen and commissioned as 2d major of Col. Mason Wheaton's 4th Lincoln county regiment of Massachusetts militia,

February 8, 1776. Later he was promoted to the rank of major.

Major Robinson was a son of Dr. Moses Robinson who came to Cushing about the year 1743. He married Priscilla Hyler by whom he had the following children:

1. Priscilla, married a Gardner; resided and died in Cushing.

2. Margaret, born in 1763; married John Rokes of Warren where she resided until her death April 19, 1806. Mr. Rokes was born March 5, 1773; died Aug. 9, 1854.

3. Simeon, married Hannah Hyler; resided in Cushing.

4. Agnes, married, first, Caleb Howard; second, Robert Porterfield; removed to Ohio.

5. Betsey, married Cornelius Hyler; resided and died in Cushing.

6. Hanse, 2d, married Lucy Hyler; resided and died in Cushing.

7. Moses, 5th, married Priscilla Hyler; resided in Cushing, and was drowned June, 1833, from the sloop Orient on the passage from Bangor to Rockland.

8. John, 4th, married Polly Dillaway; resided and died in Hope.

9. Thomas, married a Collamore; resided and died in Hope.

10. Jacob, married, first, Nancy (or, as the town records have it, Anameriah) Robinson, who died Oct. 28, 1795; second, Sarah Kelloch, born Dec. 11, 1796; died April 6, 1813.

ROBINSON, JACOB. He served as a private in Capt. Samuel Gregg's company, Col. James Cargill's regiment, from August 25, 1775, to Dec. 31, 1775. The company was raised in St. Georges, Waldoboro and Camden and stationed there for defense of the sea coast. He re-entered the service March 5, 1776, as a private in Capt. Benjamin Plummer's company and served until Dec. 10, 1776, when he was discharged. The company was stationed at St. Georges for the defense of the sea coast.

ROBINSON, JAMES. He served as sergeant in Capt. Archibald McAllister's company, Col. Samuel McCobb's regiment in the expedition against Castine from July 11, 1777, to Sept. 24, 1777.

ROBINSON, JOHN. He served as sergeant in Capt. Samuel

Gregg's company, Col. James Cargill's regiment, stationed at St. Georges, Waldoboro and Camden for the defense of the sea coast from August 8, 1775, to Dec. 31, 1775.

ROBINSON, JOSEPH. He served as a private in Capt. Starrett's detachment from Col. Mason Wheaton's regiment from June 29, 1779, to July 2, 1779, in the Eastern Department in Camden.

ROBINSON, REUBEN. He enlisted as a private in Capt. Benjamin Plummer's company, March 5, 1776, and was discharged Dec. 10, 1776. The company was stationed at St. Georges for the defense of the sea coast.

ROBINSON, ROBERT. He served as a private in Capt. Samuel Gregg's company, Col. James Cargill's regiment, from August 25, 1775, to December 31, 1775. The company was raised in St. Georges, Waldoboro and Camden and stationed there for defense of the sea coast. He joined Capt. Benjamin Plummer's company as a private March 5, 1776, and was discharged December 16, 1776. The company was stationed at St. Georges for defense of the sea coast.

ROUNDY, AZOR. On Sept. 25, 1775, a receipt was given to Daniel Hopkins at Beverly, Mass., by Azor Roundy and others for advance payment for one month's service in defense of the sea coast. He enlisted July 15, 1775, as a drummer in Capt. Moses Brown's company, serving six months and two days. The company was stationed at Beverly for defense of the sea coast. He enlisted in Capt. Jonathan Proctor's company, Col. Jacob Gerrish's regiment, Nov. 12, 1777, and served until April 3, 1778, the company being stationed at Charlestown and Cambridge, Mass. Mr. Roundy was a resident of St. Georges in 1790. He married Lydia Thorndike who was born May 22, 1757. She was a daughter of Ebenezer Thorndike and sister of Capt. Joshua Thorndike.

SEAVEY, ELIAKIM. He served as a private in Lieut. Joseph McLellan's company at the Eastward from Dec. 6, 1780, to March 24, 1781, when he was discharged. The company was detached from Col. Joseph Prime's regiment by order of Gen. Wadsworth to serve out the balance of eight months' term of enlistment.

SEAVEY, JOSEPH. He was a captain in Col. Benjamin Foster's regiment serving at Machias from Dec. 5, 1778, to Dec. 25, 1778. Members of the family residing in New Hampshire claim that Capt. Seavey was with Washington's army at Valley Forge. Capt. Seavey was born in

Portsmouth, N. H., June 12, 1747, died in Cushing, Oct. 15, 1826. He was married to Elizabeth Knight at Portsmouth, Dec. 23, 1772. On Dec. 8, 1801, Nathaniel Vickery of St. George conveyed to Capt. Seavey Georges island, containing 50 acres, on which he made his home until he settled in Cushing. The following children were born of his marriage:

1. Joseph, 2d, born Portsmouth, N. H., Dec. 14, 1774; died Cushing, July 25, 1855; married on Georges island, July 30, 1798.

2. Eunice, born May 10, 1776; married James Teel. She committed suicide at Georges island by drowning, June 3, 1816.

3. John, born Sept. 10, 1780; died Cushing, June 22, 1829; married Thankful Smalley of St. George.

4. Daniel, born Feb. 28, 1782; died St. George, Nov. 13, 1854; married Sally Smalley, Oct. 8, 1807.

5. Stephen, born Jan. 24, 1784; died St. George, Aug. 2, 1859; married Jean Hathorn.

6. Nathaniel, born Jan. 20, 1786; died St. George, March 18, 1861; married Miriam Clark.

7. Thomas, born Sept. 9, 1788; died Cushing, Feb. 18, 1849; married Mary Kerby, the ceremony performed by Col. Benjamin Burton. She was born in Cushing, Jan. 6, 1783.

8. David, born Dec. 17, 1790; died St. George, Nov. 17, 1865; married Watie Jameson.

SMITH, JOHN. He served as a private in Capt. Joseph Jones' detachment of militia; marched June 29, 1779 and was discharged July 16, 1779, at Camden, by order of Col. William Jones.

SMITH, JOHN. He served as a private in Capt. Benjamin Plummer's company from July 6, 1779, to Sept. 24, 1779, on the Penobscot expedition. The company was detached from Col. William Jones' regiment for service under Col. Samuel McCobb on an expedition against Majorbagaduce.

SMITH, WILLIAM. He entered the service as lieutenant in Capt. Nicholas Crosby's company, Col. Samuel McCobb's regiment Aug. 2, 1777. The certificate on the roll, sworn to at Penobscot, certified that the company was raised for expedition against St. John's river, N. S., for the term of six months, and was in readiness to enter on said service until discharge, Sept. 4, 1777. He also saw service as 2d lieutenant, Capt. Nicholas Crosby's company, Col. John Allen's regiment, from Oct. 7, 1777, to Dec. 31, 1777. The regiment was raised for the defense of Machias. On April 29, 1780, a William Smith enlisted as a private in Capt. Thomas Bragdon's company, Lieut. Col. Joseph Prime's regiment, and was discharged Dec. 5, 1780. Service was under Brig. Gen. Wadsworth at the Eastward. The company was reported as having marched to Thomaston.

STERLING, JOSIAH. He served as a private in Capt. Benjamin Plummer's company, stationed at St. Georges for the defense of the sea coast, from Feb. 4, 1776, to Dec. 10, 1776.

STONE, JOHN. He enlisted as a private in Capt. Jonathan Andrew's company, Col. Joseph Prime's regiment, under Brig. Gen. Wadsworth at the Eastward, and served from May 8, 1780, to Oct. 9, 1780. The roll was sworn to in York County and certified at Thomaston.

STOVER, CHRISTOPHER. He enlisted Jan. 1, 1776, at Harpswell as a private in Capt. Wilde's company, Col. Phinney's Massachusetts regiment, Continental line, serving eleven months, when he went home on a furlough on condition that he enlist again for three years. On Jan. 1, 1777, he enlisted, as promised, in Capt. Daniel Merrill's company, Col. Samuel McCobb's Massachusetts regiment, Continental line, and served the whole three years in Capt. Merrill's company, Gen. Patterson's brigade. Mr. Stover was in the battles resulting in the surrender of Burgoyne's army at Saratoga. He died at Appleton, Sept. 8, 1828, leaving a widow, Catherine.

SWEETLAND, JAMES. He served as a private in Capt. Benjamin Plummer's company, stationed at St. Georges for the defense of the sea coast, from Feb. 4, 1776, to Dec. 10, 1776.

Mr. Sweetland married Hannah, one of the five daughters of Rev. Robert Rutherford, a Presbyterian minister and the first one of that faith to preach in Maine. Mr. Rutherford purchased lots, 56, 57 and 58 situated on the western side of St. Georges river, each containing 100 acres, from Gen. Samuel Waldo of Boston, grandfather of the wife of Gen. Henry Knox, Jan. 26, 1743. These lots are on the road leading to Hathorn's point, lying between the Oliver Kerby farm on the north and the Hathorn farm on the south. The middle lot, known as the Taylor place, is now owned by William L. McNamara of Bangor, formerly of Thomaston, and occupied by him as a summer home. Mrs. Sweetland's first husband was a McFarland. Mr. Sweetland died in Cushing, Sept. 30, 1804, at the age of 63 years. His wife died March, 1820, aged 79, and is buried in Pleasant Point cemetery.

THORNDIKE, JOSHUA, CAPTAIN. He enlisted immediately after the battle of Bunker Hill, at first for six months and then for three years, joining the army at Cambridge. Subsequently engaging on board a privateer fitted out at Falmouth, he was soon captured by the British sloop Albany, and detained a prisoner on board for nine months. The sloop afterwards foundered on the Triangles, a part of the Mussel Ridge Group and a short distance north of Little Green island.

Capt. Thorndike was born March 12, 1755, and died Dec. 2, 1824, and is buried on the John Foster farm, South Thomaston. He lived for a short time on Metinic island but most of his life was spent at St. George. On Aug. 23, 1780, he married Hannah Nutting, a daughter of Jonathan Nutting of Cushing. She was born June 21, 1764; died Jan. 12, 1852.

The following children were born to Joshua and Hannah Thorndike:

1. Bethiah, born May 23, 1781; married first, Capt. William Keating, Feb. 19, 1800. He resided at South Thomaston, and died at Havana, of yellow fever. Her second husband was Thomas Martin of St. George, who later in life resided in South Thomaston.

2. Capt. Joshua, 2d, born April 3, 1787; married Susan Keating, a daughter of Dea. Richard Keating, March 19, 1812. She was born Feb. 22, 1794; died March 21, 1863.

3. Hannah, born July 16, 1789; married Capt. Robert Snow, 2d. He was born in 1788; died Aug. 28, 1848.

4. Eben, born Aug. 26, 1791; died September, 1852; married Elizabeth, daughter of Capt. Robert Snow.

5. George, born March 31, 1793; died at Turk's island, 1815.

6. Eliza, born Jan. 4, 1799; died September, 1803.

VICKERY, BENJAMIN. He enlisted as a private in Capt. Samuel McCobb's regiment, Col. Joseph Reed's regiment, May 8, 1775, and served three months and one day.

MAINE SOLDIERS AND SAILORS

VOSE, SETH. He was a sergeant in Capt. Thomas Starrett's detachment from Col. Mason Wheaton's regiment serving from June 29, 1779, to July 2, 1779, at Camden in the Eastern Department.

Mr. Vose was the son of Jonathan Vose of Milton, Mass., and was born Jan. 4, 1733 or '34. He came to Maine in 1763 and on the 18th of September, 1765, he purchased of Alexander McDowell, a cooper, of Worcester, Mass., lot No. 4, situated on the west side of St. Georges river, in Cushing. He married Rachel Copeland of Warren, daughter of David and Elizabeth Copeland. She was born Feb. 12, 1749.

The following children were born of this marriage:

1. Elijah, born Aug. 1, 1776; died April 10, 1840; married Sarah Andrews who was born Sept. 14, 1767; died Nov. 19, 1840.

2. Mary, born 1770; married first, John McIntyre, 2d, who was born in 1761; resided in Warren and died Aug. 18, 1814; second, Dea. Calvin Crane in 1816; resided in Hope and Warren. He died March, 1843, aged about 80 years.

3. Seth, 2d, born 1772; married Lydia Delano, and died Oct. 18, 1846.

4. Ebenezer, born 1774; married first, Nancy Lermond, Jan. 14, 1802. She was born Jan. 28, 1781; died April 17, 1811. He married, second, Sarah (Bridges) Dunbar, May 9, 1812; resided in Thomaston a while, then removed to Montville where he died May 21, 1829.

5. David, born Feb. 8, 1776; married Alice L. Eastman; removed to Montville, and died Feb. 25, 1844.

6. Elizabeth, married Capt. Archibald Robinson, 3d, who was born Jan. 8, 1783. He resided in Cushing, and died in the West Indies.

7. Hannah, married Dr. Josiah Cushing a graduate of Harvard University in the class of 1798. She died Oct. 24, 1816. Dr. Cushing came from Scituate, Mass., or vicinity, and practiced medicine in Thomaston and Nobleboro. Intentions of marriage were published April 23, 1808. He died in Thomaston, in 1819.

8. Rufus, died young.

9. William, married Jane McCarter, April 7, 1814. She was born May 18, 1788.

10. John, born 1784; died in Cushing, May 7, 1839; married first, Mary Hyler, Aug. 11, 1816; second, Hannah S. Healey, December, 1834. She was born Dec. 9, 1799; died Dec. 8, 1860.

WALL, ANDREW. He served as a private in Capt. Archibald McAllister's company, Col. Prime's regiment, under Brig. Gen. Wadsworth at the Eastward, and served from April 23, 1780 to Dec. 14, 1780 when he was discharged. The roll was certified to at Headquarters, Thomaston.

WATTS, SAMUEL. He was a private in Lieut. Joel Whitney's company, which was a part of the Lincoln County regiment under the command of Col. Benjamin Foster. He served from July 16, 1777, to the date of discharge, Oct. 7, 1777, during which time the company was stationed at Machias. Mr. Watts was born on Long Island, a son of William Watts who came to this country in the Scotch Irish emigration of 1719. He married Mary Robinson, daughter of Moses Robinson, 2d, of Cushing, Dec. 22, 1772.

At the first town meeting held in Cushing in 1789 it was voted to build two town pounds for the impounding of stray animals, one on the Cushing side of the river on Archibald Robinson's farm, with Mr. Robinson as pound keeper, and the other on the St. Georges side on Mr. Watts' premises, with Mr. Watts as pound keeper. At this meeting Mr. Watts was elected one of the selectmen and one of the fish wardens. In 1790 he was elected church warden and pound keeper, and at a special meeting held April 27, he was appointed with others as a committee to settle accounts for and against the town. From this year until 1803, when St. George was incorporated, he held several town offices. Mr. Watts resided and died in St. George where his children were born.

1. Joseph, born Sept. 27, 1773, married first, Sarah Stone of Lincolnville; second, Cynthia (Everett) Ranlett. He died in St. George, Sept. 7, 1841.

2. Margaret, born, July 27, 1775; married Moses Fogerty of St. George.

3. Jane, born June 23, 1777; married Joshua Smalley.

4. John, born March 20, 1779, a master mariner; married Hannah Smalley.

5. Samuel, 2d, born April 12, 1781; died at Guadaloupe from a cut and ensuing mortification.

6. Moses, born June 5, 1783; married first, Catherine McKeller; second, Polly Fogerty; removed and died in Montville.

7. Mary, born July 11, 1785; died with diphtheria.

8. William, born Dec. 11, 1787; married Jane, daughter of Thomas Henderson of St. George; resided in Thomaston, a carpenter, militia officer and so forth.

9. George, born March 16, 1790; married Mary Giles of St. George

10. Elizabeth, born July 20, 1792; married Asa Harrington who resided and died in Appleton.

11. Sarah, born April 2, 1795; married first, Paul Giles; second, Mark Gay of Cushing. She resided and died in Thomaston, November, 1859. Mr. Gay was born June 2, 1800; died April 3, 1871.

WELLS, JOHN. He enlisted as a private in Capt. Benjamin Plummer's company, Sept. 5, 1776, and was discharged Dec. 10, 1776. The company was stationed at St. Georges for defense of the sea coast.

WILEY, EPHRAIM. He enlisted as a private in Capt. Samuel Gregg's company, James Cargill's regiment, Aug. 25, 1775, and was discharged Dec. 31, 1775. The company was raised in St. Georges, Waldoboro and Camden and stationed there for defense of the sea coast. His name appears among the list of men mustered by Nathaniel Barter, muster master for Suffolk County, dated at Boston, March 16, 1777, as a member of Capt. Wiley's company, Col. Jackson's regiment, and was reported as having received State bounty. Mr. Wiley was promoted to the rank of corporal in Capt. John Wiley's company, Col. Michael Jackson's regiment, the Continental army pay accounts showing service from Feb. 6, 1777, to Dec. 31, 1779. He was a sergeant in Capt. Pierce's company, Col. Jackson's regiment, and according to the Continental army pay accounts he served from Jan. 1, 1780, to Dec. 31, 1780. In the descriptive list of the members of Capt. Pierce's 6th company, 8th Massachusetts regiment, commanded by Col. Michael Jackson, his rank is given as sergeant; age, 21 years; stature, five feet and ten inches; complexion, light; hair, black; occupation, yeoman; birthplace Townsend; residence St. Georges. On Jan. 1, 1777, he was engaged by Capt. Wiley at Boston to remain in the service during the war. He was with the army at Valley Forge during the memorable winter of 1777. At the time he applied for a pension, he had resided in St. George for 75 years. Mr. Wiley married Susanna Collamore of Meduncook, the intentions of marriage being filed with the clerk of Cushing, Nov. 12, 1791.

WILEY, ISAAC. He was commissioned July 2, 1778 as captain of the 5th company of Col. Wheaton's 4th Lincoln county regiment of Massachusetts. According to the census of 1790 Mr. Wiley was a resident of St. George, his family consisting of ten members. One of his daughters, Eliza, married Andrew Malcolm of Cushing, son of James Malcolm, a noted land surveyor. Mrs. Malcolm was the grandmother of Mrs. Charles A. Creighton of Thomaston.

WILEY, WILLIAM. He served as a private in Capt. Benjamin Lemont's company, Col. McCobb's regiment, at the Eastward in 1781. He resided in Cushing.

WILLIS, THOMAS. He served three years in Col. Brooks' Massachusetts regiment, enlisting from Topsfield, Mass. He died in St. George, Jan. 19, 1795, having resided there the last nine years of his life. His wife, Joanna, survived him.

YOUNG, ALEXANDER. He enlisted as a private in Capt. Samuel Gregg's company, Col. Cargill's regiment, Aug. 25, 1775, and was discharged Dec. 31, 1775. The company was raised in St. Georges, Waldoboro and Camden, and stationed there in defense of the sea coast. On July 7, 1779, he signed shipping articles as a seaman with several others to serve on board the sloop "Industry," Capt. William Young, master, bound on a voyage from Boston to Penobscot and return. Mr. Young's name was included in a list of men belonging to the several transports engaged in the Penobscot expedition, according to the roll made up agreeable to a resolve of March 23, 1784, attested by Joshua Davis, agent. He was reported as belonging to the sloop "Industry." He died Nov. 9, 1820, at the age of 62 years, and is buried in Pleasant Point cemetery.

YOUNG, FRANCIS. He enlisted as a private in Capt. Samuel Gregg's company, James Cargill's regiment, August 25, 1775, and was discharged Dec. 31, 1775. The company was raised in St. Georges and Waldoboro and stationed there for the defense of the sea coast. He re-enlisted in Capt. Jacob Ludwig's company Oct. 7, 1777, and was discharged

Dec. 22, 1777, the company being raised for the defense of Machias. Mr. Young was allowed 200 miles travel from Machias to his home, and ten days' extra pay for loss of time. He was promoted to corporal in Capt. Philip M. Ulmer's company, Col. Samuel McCobb's regiment, serving from July 8, 1779, to Sept. 24, 1779, on the Penobscot expedition. Mr. Young was born in Cushing in 1750; died in North Warren, April 7, 1834. He married Margaret Kelloch, eldest daughter of Alexander Kelloch of Warren. She was born in 1766; died June 17, 1826. On May 28, 1779, Mr. Young purchased of his father, Robert Young, the homestead premises, designated as lot No. 5 on the Waldo plan. This lot contained 50 acres, and was situated on the west side of St. Georges river, adjoining premises of Seth Vose, now of Edwin S. Vose, on the north, and premises of Jonathan Nutting on the south. His children were:

1. William, married Mary Davis, Aug. 16, 1804; resided and died in Warren.

2. Mary, married first, Barnabas Simmons; second, a Wade; died at Moosehead Lake.

3. Elizabeth, married Micah Howard of Thomaston, Feb. 26, 1809; resided and died in Washington.

4. Alexander, born Oct. 1, 1792; married Rosanna Libby, March 28, 1822; resided at North Warren and died Aug. 1, 1861.

5. Lavinia, married David Reed of Belfast, Jan. 1, 1823; removed to Minnesota, and died there May 1875.

6. Moses H., married Rosanna Grinnell; resided in Belfast and died there in 1873.

YOUNG, GEORGE. He was elected captain of the 5th company, Col. Mason Wheaton's 4th Lincoln County regiment, of the Massachusetts militia, June 3, 1776, and was commissioned July 3, 1776.

Very few details in the family history of Mr. Young are obtainable. Among the list of settlers (or heads of families) in the Plantation of Lower St. Georges, compiled by Col. John North in 1760, appear the names of George Young and William Young, supposed to be brothers. George Young resided on a farm, containing 64 acres, being lot No. 64, according to the Waldo survey and plan, conveyed to him March 20, 1774 by Thomas Flucker of Boston, Isaac Winslow of Boston and Francis

OF THE REVOLUTIONARY WAR

Waldo of Falmouth. This lot was bounded on the east by Maple Juice cove, an arm of St. Georges river, and on the west by Meduncook river.

In the census returns of 1790 the names of George Young and William Young appear as residents of the lower part of Cushing, the former with a family of five and the latter with a family of six. George Young, junior, was born in 1769 and died in 1843. His wife, Anne Johnston of Bristol, was born in 1772 and died in 1856. Their intentions of marriage were filed with the town clerk of Cushing, Dec. 21, 1793. Mrs. Young was the daughter of Thomas Johnston, who left Scotland at the age of 18 years, and was one of those who went with General Waldo to Falmouth, and worked four years in payment of his passage over. He enlisted, served under Col. Henderson at the Pleasant Point garrison house during the French and Indian War, and in 1759 at Pemaquid, where he remained and settled in the present town of Bristol. Johnston was one of the selectmen for about forty years, was a commissary at St. Georges about six months in the War of the Revolution and died in 1811, leaving a numerous posterity. He was born at Longformacus, in Berwickshire, Scotland; saw the advertisement of Waldo in time of discouragement, and robbed of all his property (obtained on credit) embarked immediately without going home. He had an education superior to most of his associates in the then wilderness of Maine, and was a most useful, worthy and trusted public man and magistrate.

The children of George and Anne (Johnston) Young:

1. Mary, married William Jameson of Friendship.

2. Catherine, married Capt. George Davis.

3. Anne, died young.

4. Margaret, married Robert McIntyre, 2d.

5. Jane M., married John McIntyre, 3d, Dec. 19, 1816.

6. William, married Lucy Hahn of Waldoboro.

7. Alexander, married Charlotte Jameson.

8. George, married Elizabeth Allen, Jan. 24, 1835. He was born June 20, 1813; died Jan. 25, 1853. Mrs. Young was born Jan. 7, 1810; died May 20, 1888.

9. Eliza, married Capt. Francis Gracia.

YOUNG, WILLIAM. On July 5, 1779, he signed shipping articles as master with several others to serve on board the sloop "Industry," bound on a voyage from Boston to Penobscot and return. His name appears as master of the sloop "Industry" in the list of transports employed on the Penobscot expedition, as returned by Seth Loring, Secretary, dated at the war office July 11, 1779. Subsequently the sloop was reported lost.

He died April 18, 1794 at the age of 74 years, and is buried in Pleasant Point cemetery. On April 14, 1772, Andrew Ring Johnson of Yarmouth, Maine, conveyed to Mr. Young a lot of land lying between Maple Juice Cove on the east and Meduncook river on the west, containing 72 acres, for the sum of 57 pounds. Johnson purchased this lot of Michael and Eleanor Rolley (Rawley), May 14, 1770.

Intentions of marriage of Johnson and Margaret Adams of Meduncook, now Friendship, were published Oct. 29, 1768. Miss Adams was a daughter of Richard Adams, who was prominently identified with the military and civic affairs of his community. On Oct. 3, 1775, the plantation clerk of Meduncook received a certificate and gave a permit to Capt. Andrew Johnson "to carry a freight of wood to Newbury or Piscataway." Capt. Johnson probably died prior to 1792, as Richard Adams in his will, executed in that year, made a bequest to his daughter Margaret Young, and it is fair to assume that Capt. Johnson died and his widow remarried.

www.ingramcontent.com/pod-product-compliance
Lightning Source LLC
Chambersburg PA
CBHW060809110426
42739CB00032BA/3153